**AUTHENTIC TRANSCRIPTIONS
WITH NOTES AND TABLATURE**

ACOUSTIC ROCK GUITAR BIBLE

S0-BOF-904

ISBN 0-634-06112-7

**HAL•LEONARD®
CORPORATION**

7777 W. BLUEMOUND RD. P.O. BOX 13819 MILWAUKEE, WI 53213

Visit Hal Leonard Online at
www.halleonard.com

TABLE OF CONTENTS

About a Girl

Words and Music by Kurt Cobain

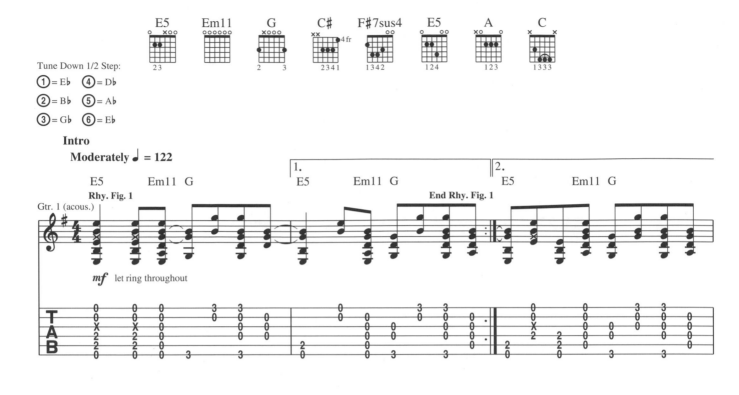

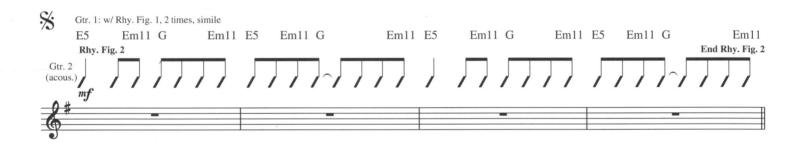

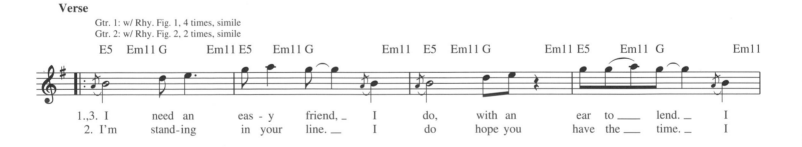

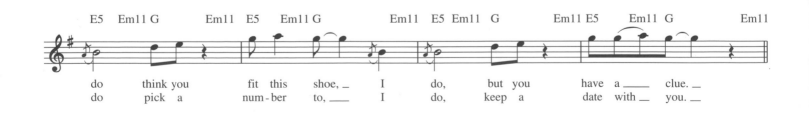

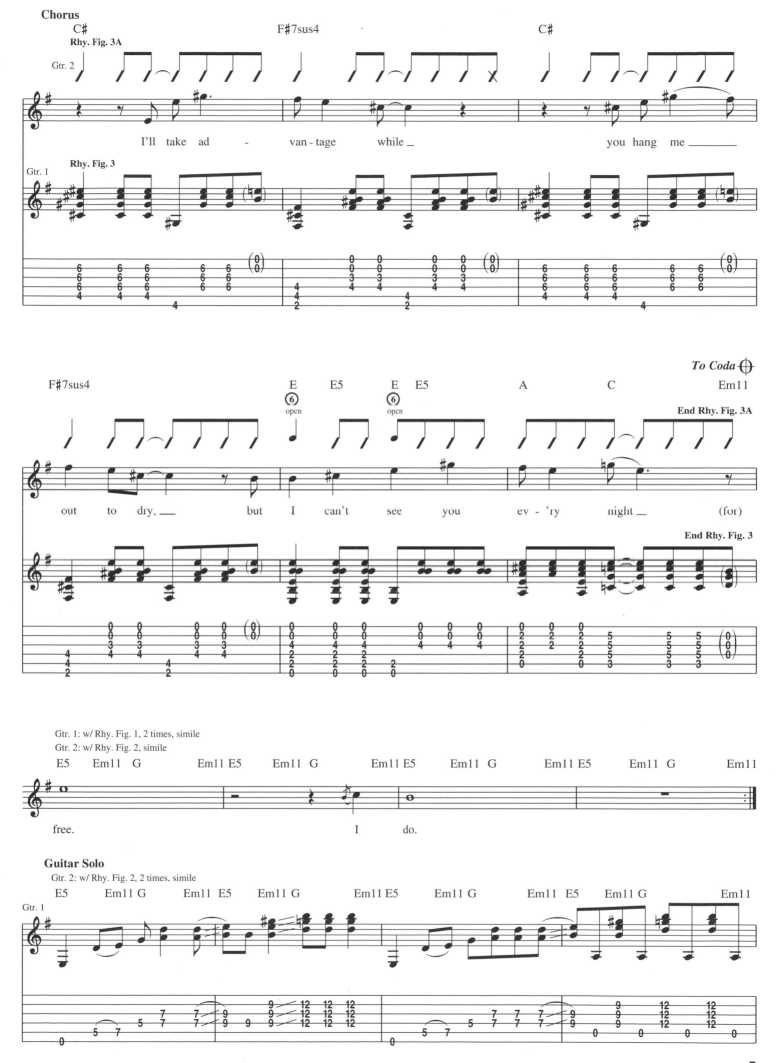

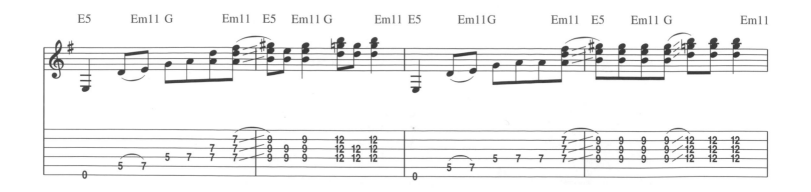

Gtrs. 1 & 2: w/ Rhy. Figs. 3 & 3A, simile

D.S. al Coda

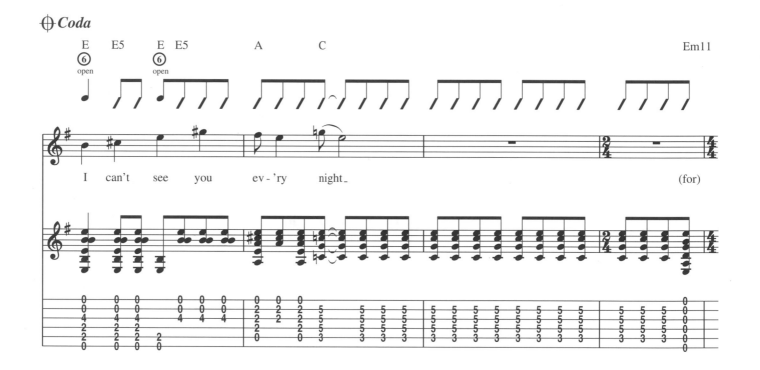

I can't see you ev-'ry night___ (for)

Gtr. 1: w/ Rhy. Fig. 1, 4 times, simile
Gtr. 2: w/ Rhy. Fig. 2, 2 times, simile

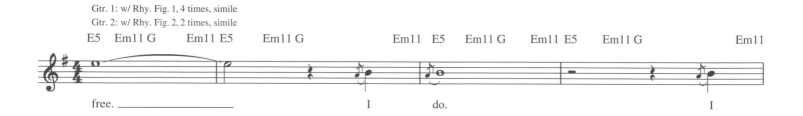

free. ___ I do. I

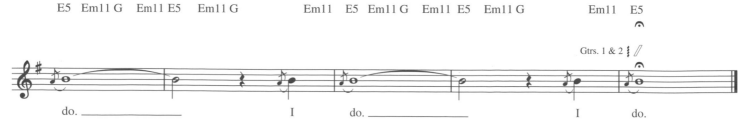

do. ___ I do. ___ I do.

And I Love Her

Words and Music by John Lennon and Paul McCartney

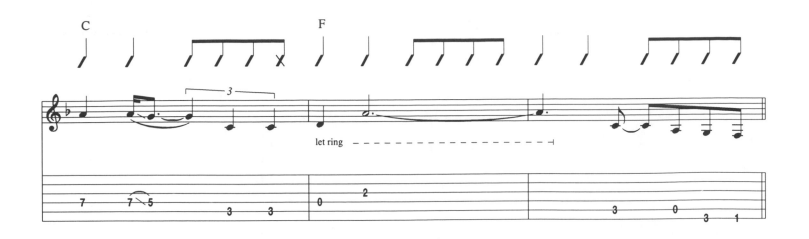

Verse

4. Bright are the stars ___ that shine, ___ dark is the sky. ___

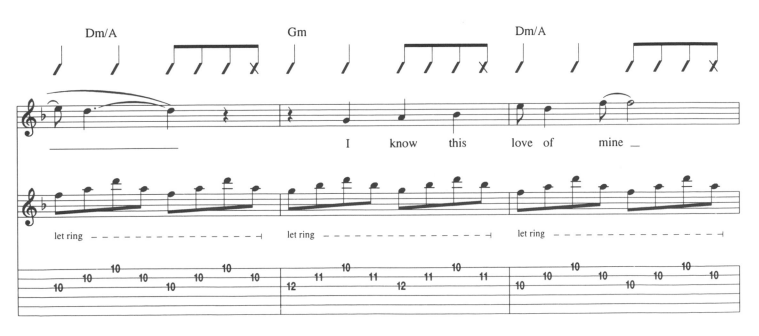

I know this love of mine ___

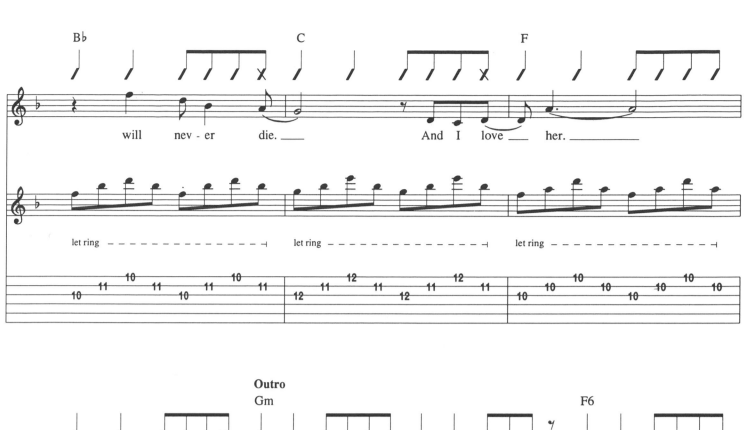

will nev-er die. _____ And I love _____ her. _____

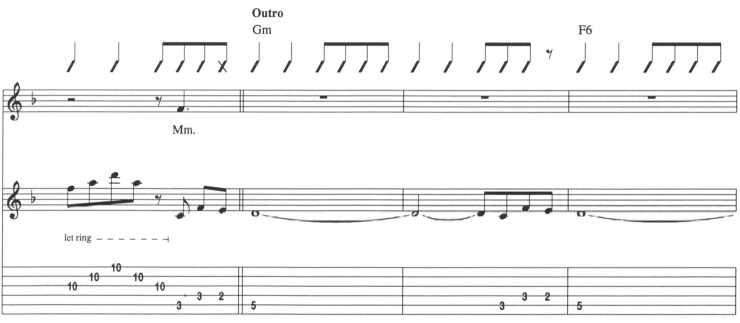

Mm.

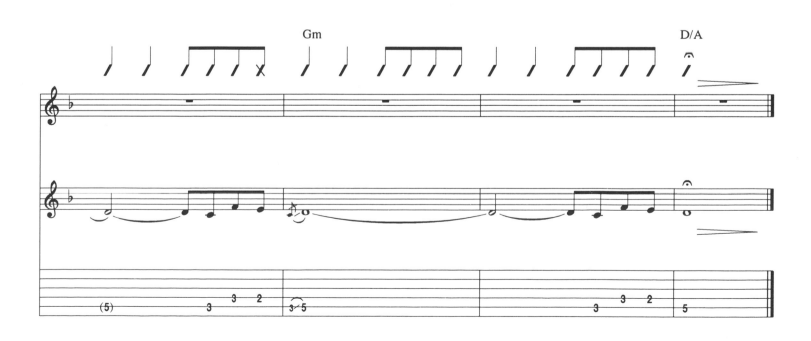

Before You Accuse Me
(Take a Look at Yourself)

Words and Music by Ellas McDaniels

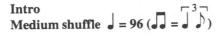

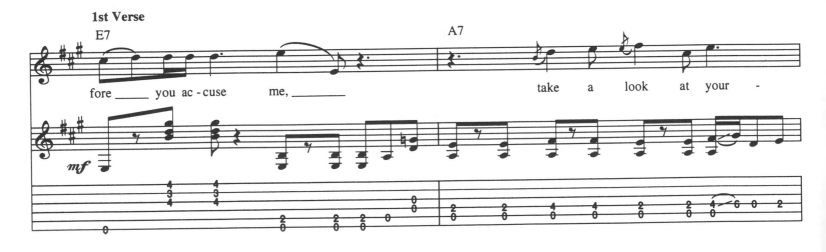

4th Verse

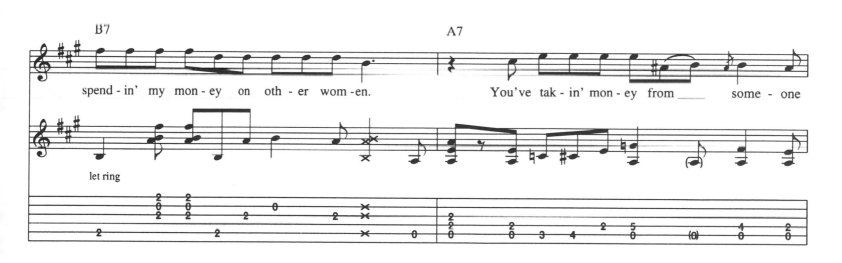

2nd Guitar Solo

Behind Blue Eyes

Words and Music by Pete Townshend

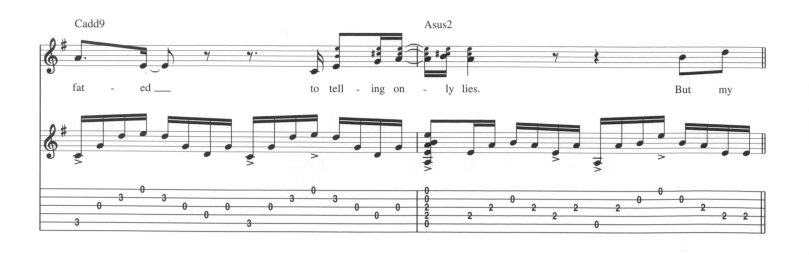

fat - ed ____ to tell - ing on - ly lies. But my

Chorus

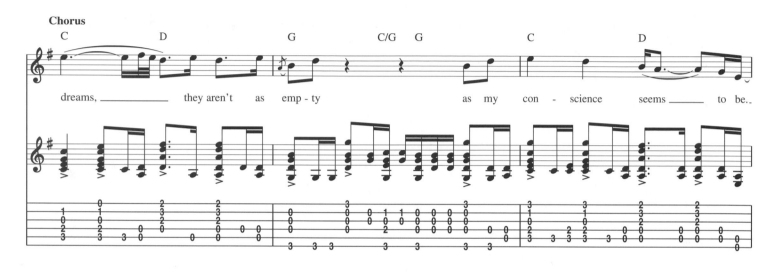

dreams, ____ they aren't as emp - ty as my con - science seems ____ to be..

____ I have hours ____ on - ly lone - ly. ____ My love is ven -

- geance that's nev - er free. 2. N -

Verse

no one knows what it's like to feel these feel - ings like I do,-
(Ah.)

and I blame you. N -
(Ah.)

no one bites back as hard on their an - ger, none of my
(Ah.)

pain and woe can show through. But my
(Ah.)

* Vibrato achieved by applying force with right hand on gtr. body & left hand on neck.

Outro
Half-Time ♩ = 60

N - no one knows what it's like __ to be the

bad man, __ to be the sad man __ be - hind __ blue eyes. __

Breaking the Girl

Words and Music by Anthony Kiedis, Flea, John Frusciante and Chad Smith

Champagne Supernova

Words and Music by Noel Gallagher

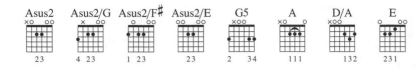

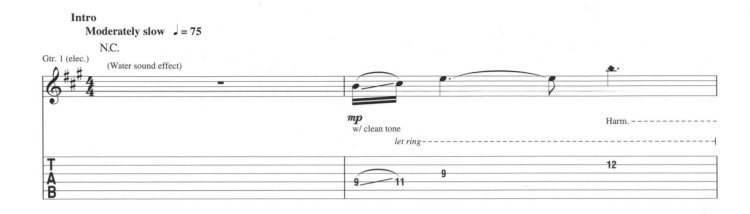

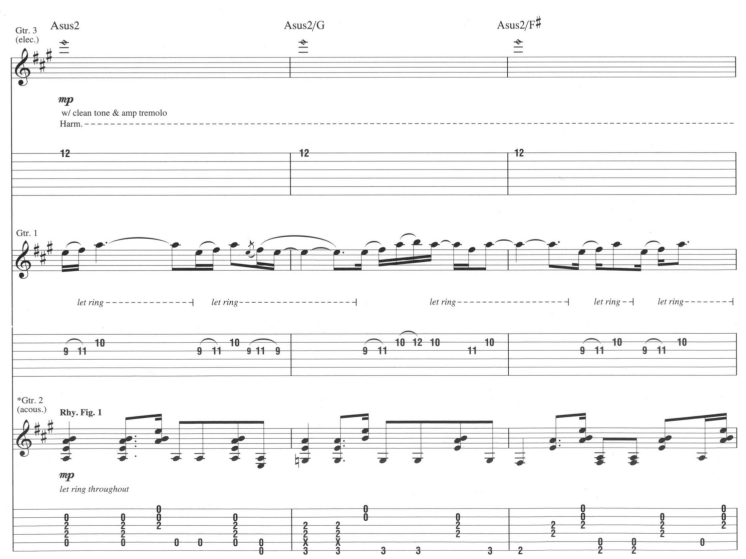

*Two gtrs. arr. for one.

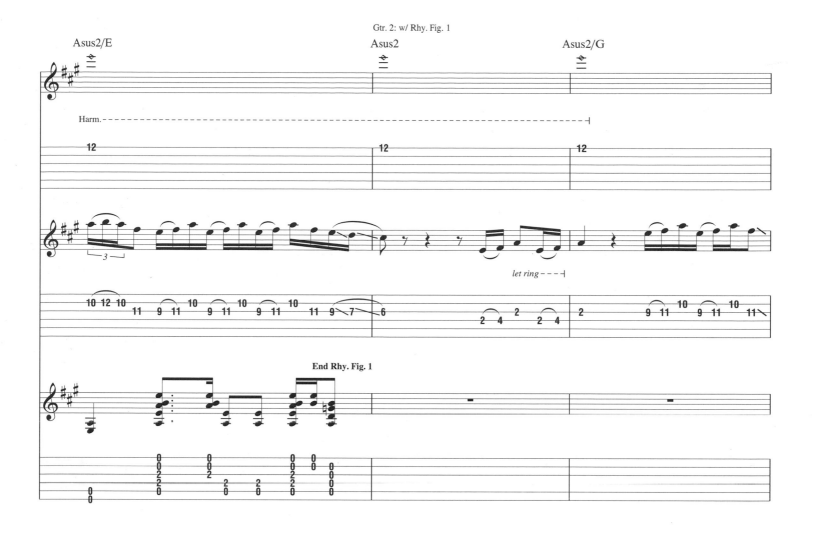

Verse

1. How man - y spe - cial peo - ple change?

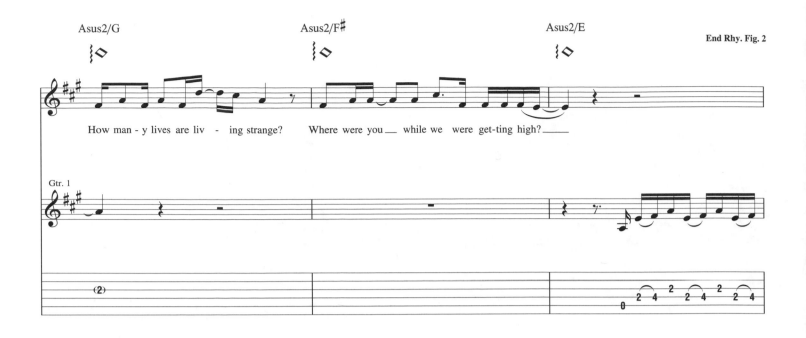

How man - y lives are liv - ing strange? Where were you __ while we were get-ting high? __

Gtr. 1

(2)

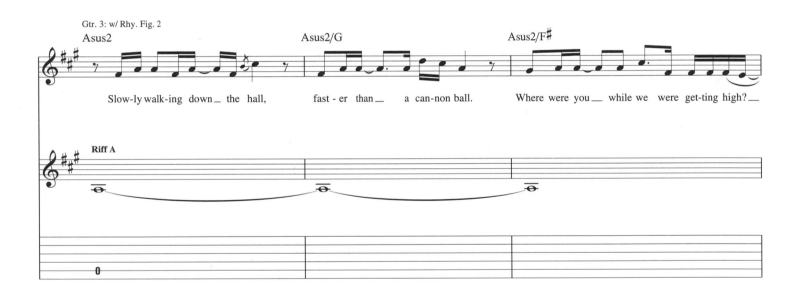

Gtr. 3: w/ Rhy. Fig. 2

Asus2   Asus2/G   Asus2/F#

Slow-ly walk-ing down __ the hall, fast - er than __ a can-non ball. Where were you __ while we were get-ting high? __

Riff A

Chorus

Gtr. 1: w/ Riff A
Gtr. 2: w/ Rhy. Fig. 1 (2 times)
Gtr. 3: w/ Rhy. Fig. 2 (1 3/4 times)

Asus2/E   Asus2   Asus2/G

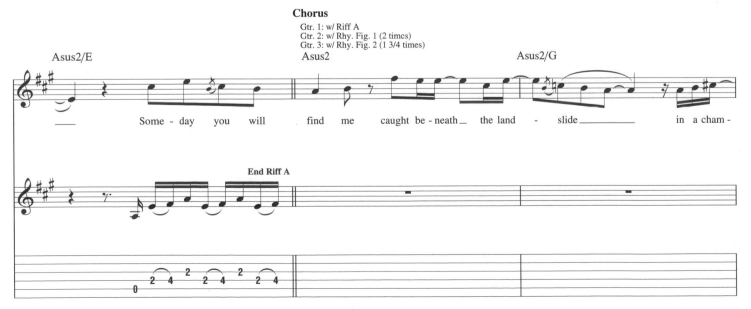

__ Some - day you will find me caught be - neath __ the land - slide __ in a cham -

End Riff A

-pagne su-per-no - va in the sky.____ Some-day you will find me caught be-neath___ the land-

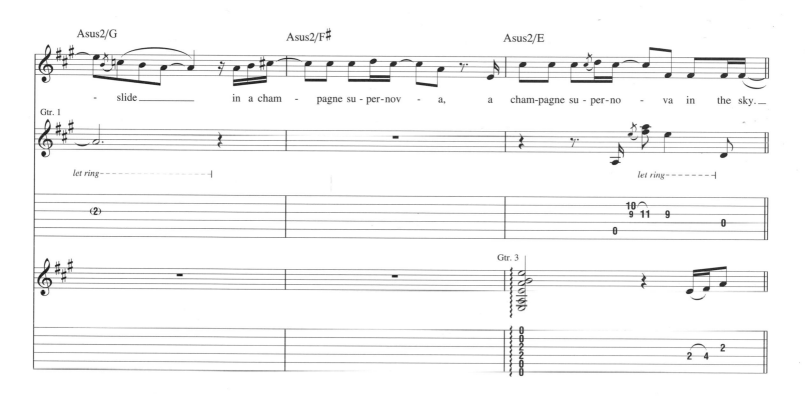

-slide_____ in a cham - pagne su-per-nov - a, a cham-pagne su-per-no - va in the sky.___

Interlude

Gtr. 2: w/ Rhy. Fig. 1

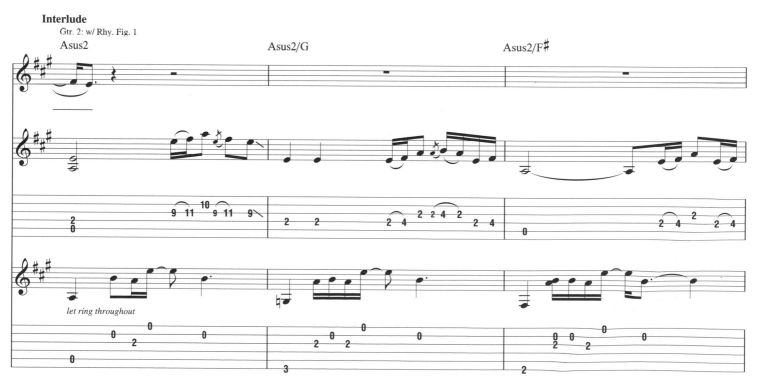

Verse

Gtr. 2: w/ Rhy. Fig. 1 (1 3/4 times)

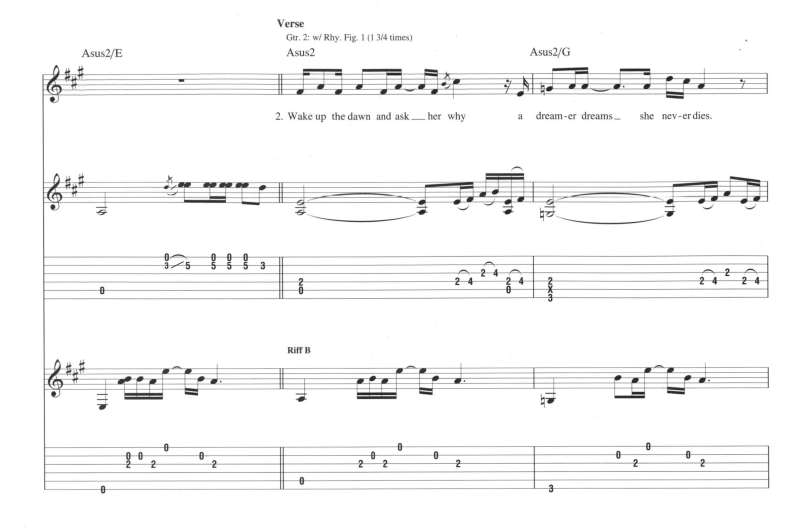

2. Wake up the dawn and ask ___ her why   a dream-er dreams ___ she nev-er dies.

Wipe that tear a - way ___   now from your eye. _____   Slow-ly walk-ing down ___   the hall,

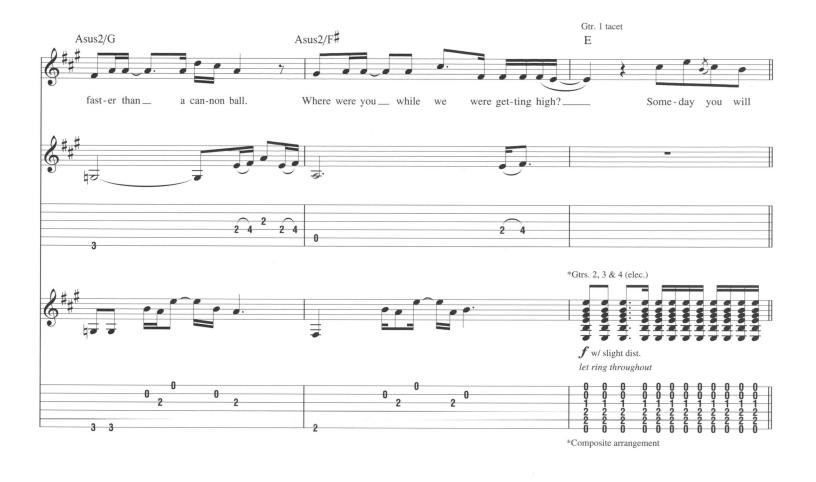

fast-er than __ a can-non ball.   Where were you __ while we   were get-ting high? __   Some-day you will

Chorus

find me caught be-neath __ the land - slide _____ in a cham - pagne su-per-no - va in the sky. __

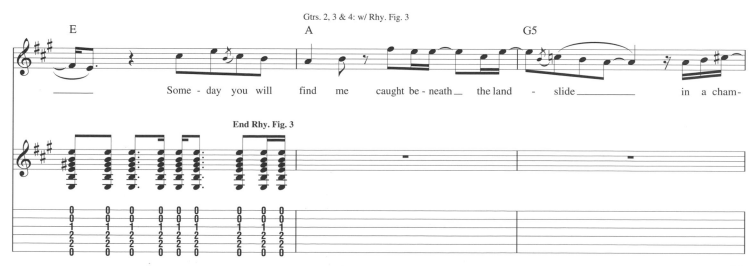

Some - day you will   find me   caught be-neath __ the land - slide _____ in a cham-

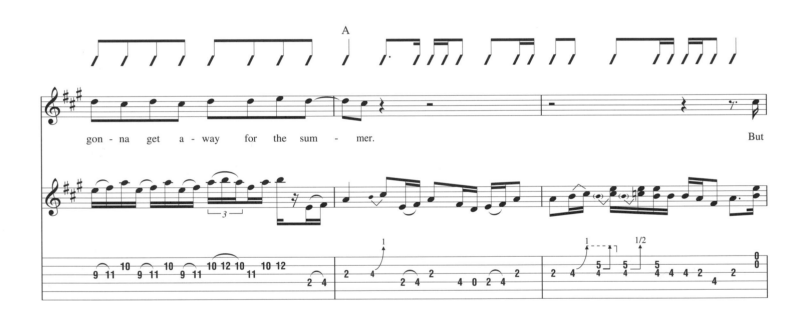

Interlude
Gtr. 2: w/ Rhy. Fig. 1 (2 times)
Gtr. 3: w/ Riff B (2 times)

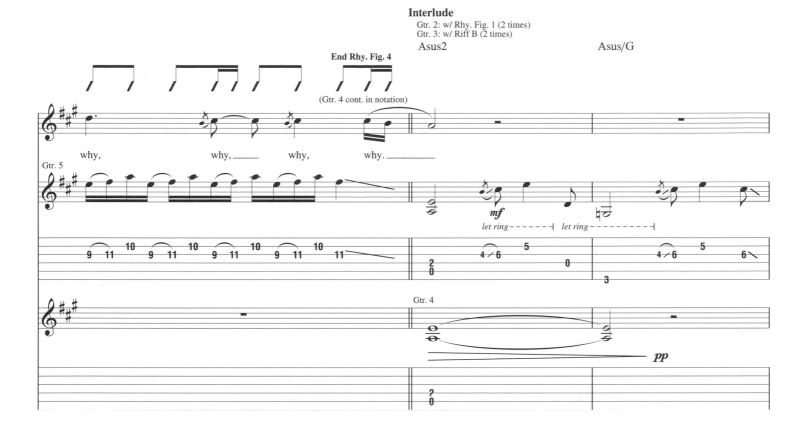

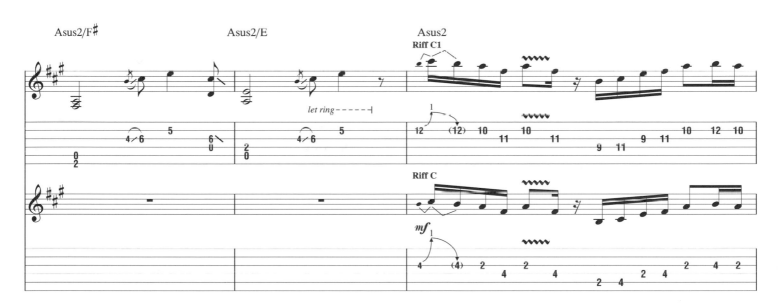

Verse

Gtr. 2: w/ Rhy. Fig. 1 (1 3/4 times)
Gtr. 3: w/ Riff B (1 3/4 times)
Gtr. 5 tacet

3. How man-y spe cial peo - ple change? How man-y lives are liv - ing strange? Where were you __ while we were get-ting high? __

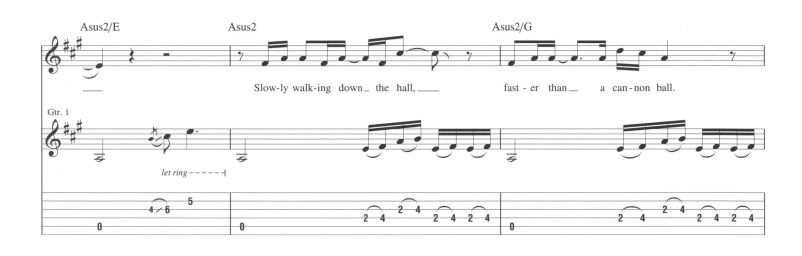

Slow-ly walk-ing down __ the hall, __ fast - er than __ a can-non ball.

Chorus

Gtr. 1 tacet
Gtrs. 2, 3 & 4: w/ Rhy. Fig. 3 (2 times)

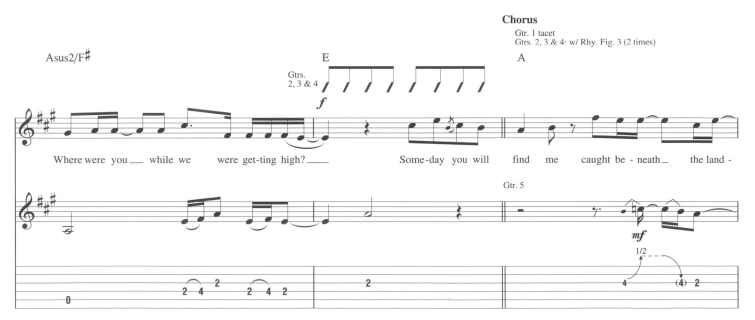

Where were you __ while we were get-ting high? __ Some-day you will find me caught be - neath __ the land -

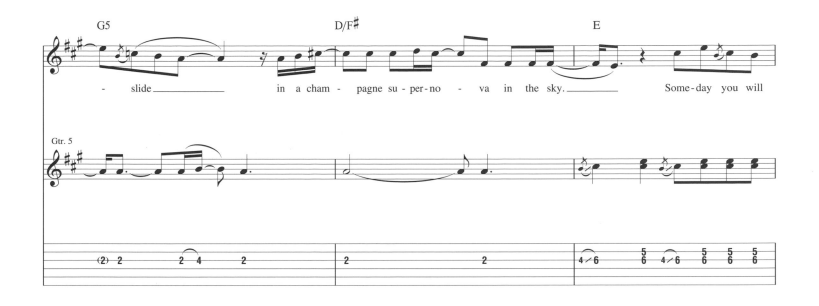

-slide _____ in a cham - pagne su - per - no - va in the sky. _____ Some-day you will

find me caught be - neath ___ the land - slide _____ in a cham - pagne su - per - no - va, a

Bridge

Gtrs. 2, 3 & 4: w/ Rhy. Fig. 4

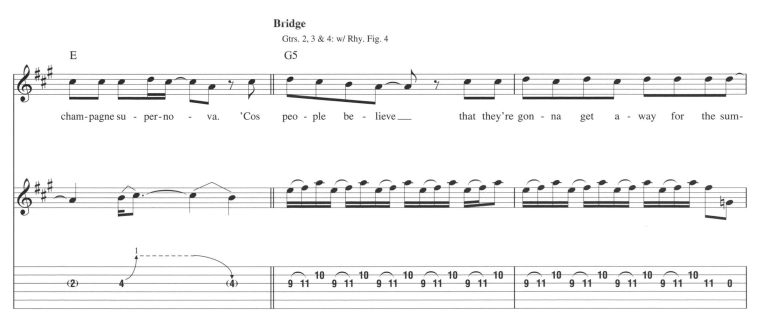

cham-pagne su - per - no - va. 'Cos peo - ple be - lieve ___ that they're gon - na get a - way for the sum-

-mer.   But you and I, _____ we live and die. The

world's still spin-ning 'round, _ we don't _ know why, _____ why, why, _ why, why. _

Guitar Solo

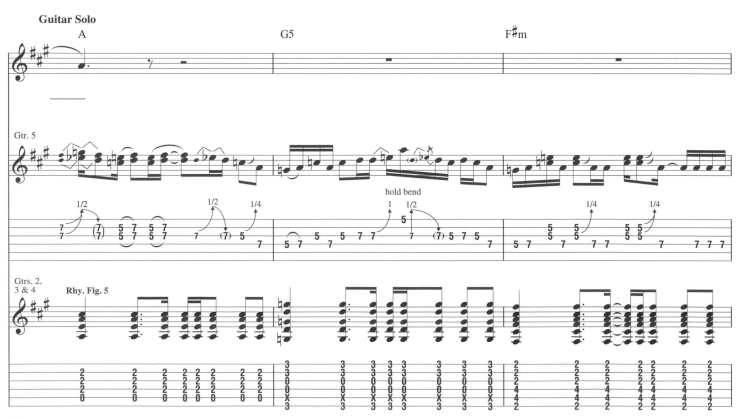

40

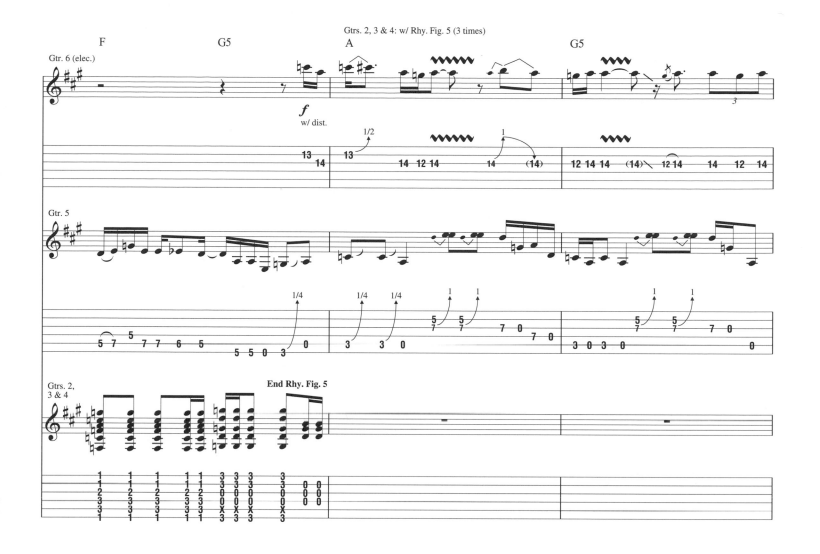

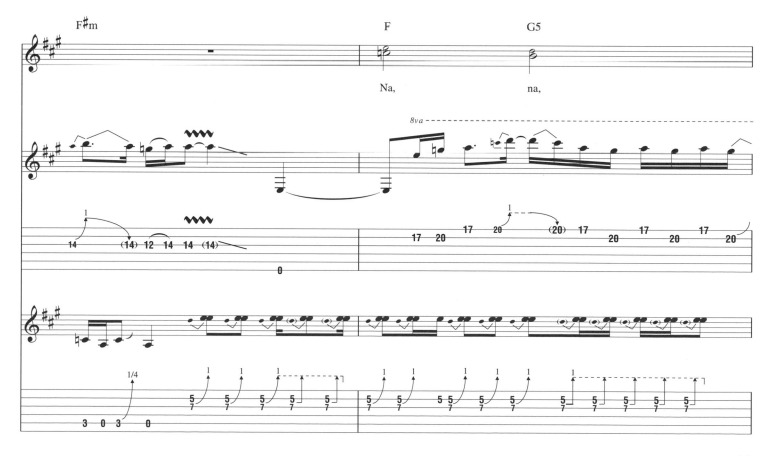

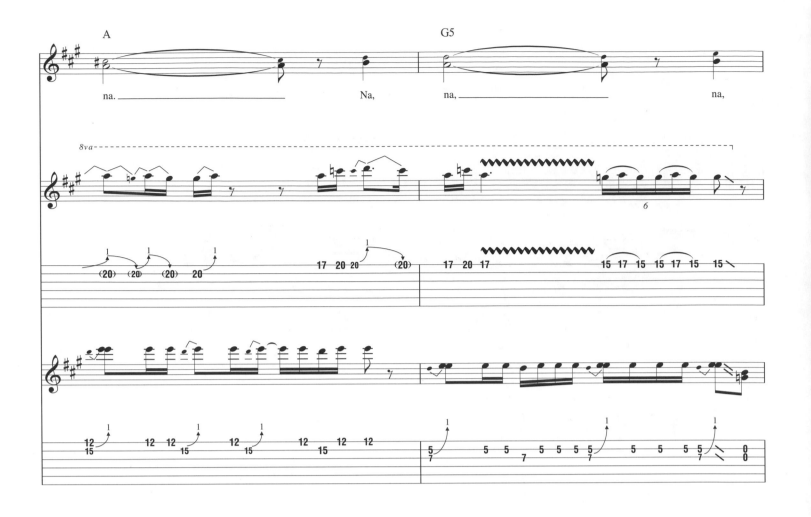

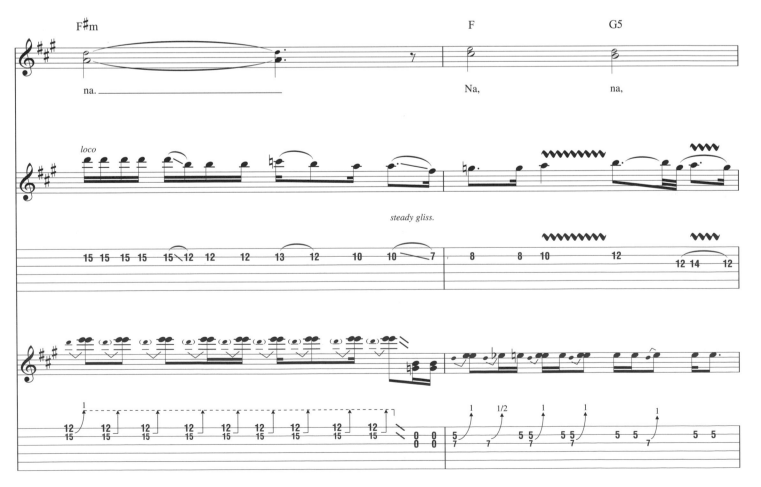

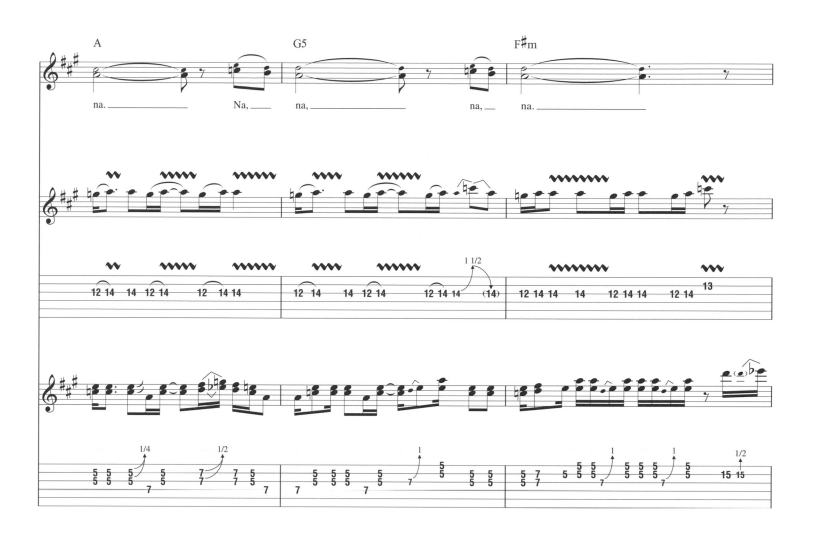

Gtrs. 2, 3 & 4: w/ Rhy. Fig. 5, last meas (2 times)

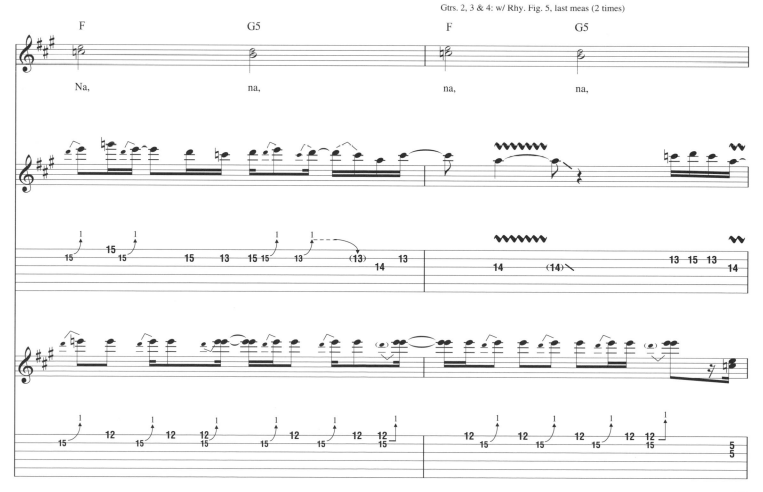

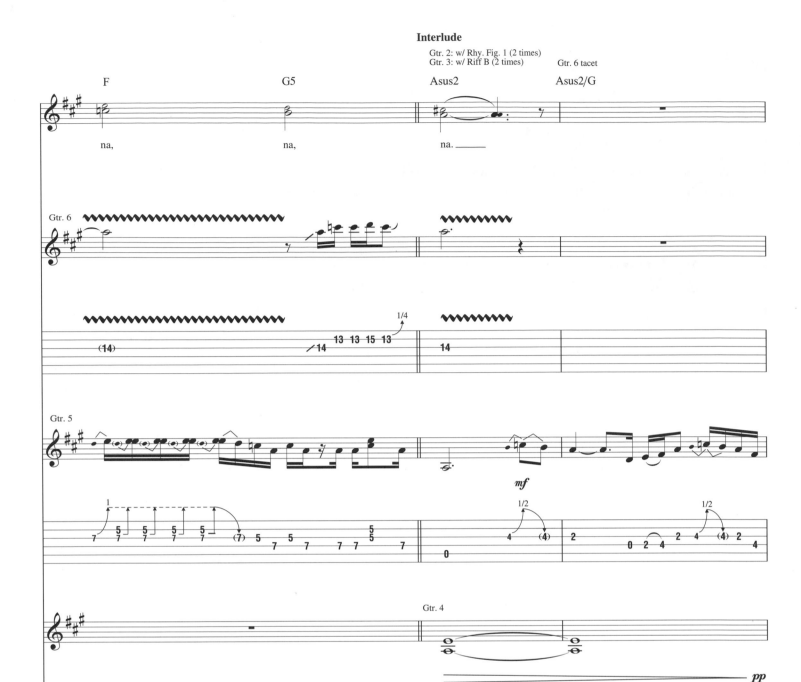

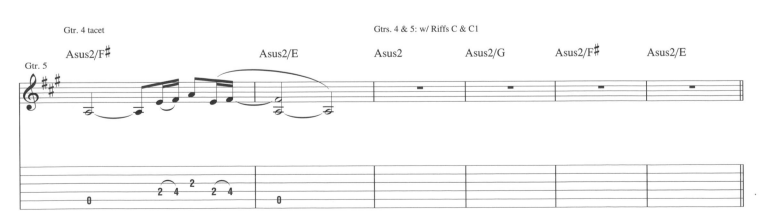

Verse

Gtr. 2: w/ Rhy. Fig. 1 (3 times)
Gtr. 3: w/ Riff B (3 times)

Gtr. 4 tacet

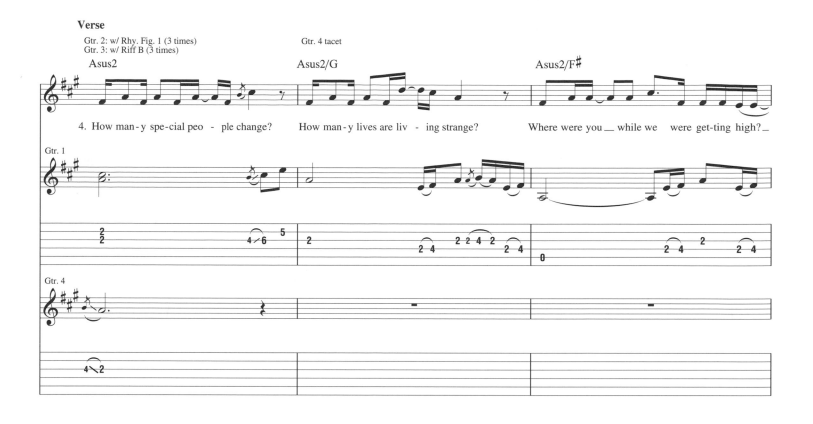

4. How man-y spe-cial peo - ple change? How man-y lives are liv - ing strange? Where were you __ while we were get-ting high? __

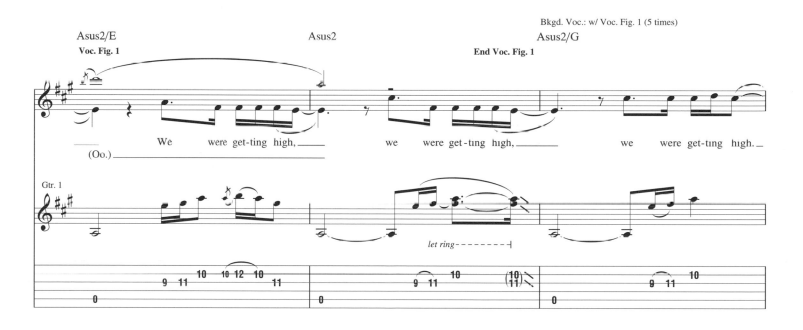

Bkgd. Voc.: w/ Voc. Fig. 1 (5 times)

Voc. Fig. 1

End Voc. Fig. 1

We were get-ting high, _____ we were get-ting high, _____ we were get-ting high. __

(Oo.)

We were get-ting high, _____ we were get-ting high, _____ we were get-ting high. __

We were get-ting high, ____ we were get-ting high, ____ we were get-ting high. ____

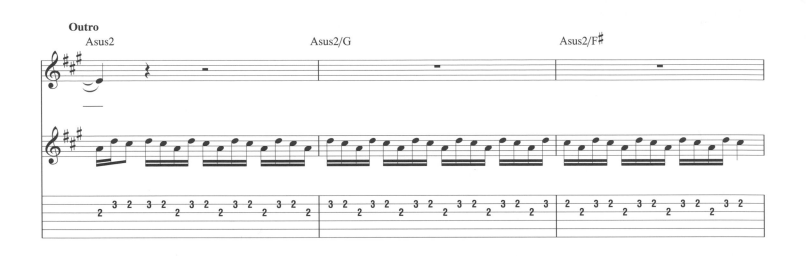

Outro

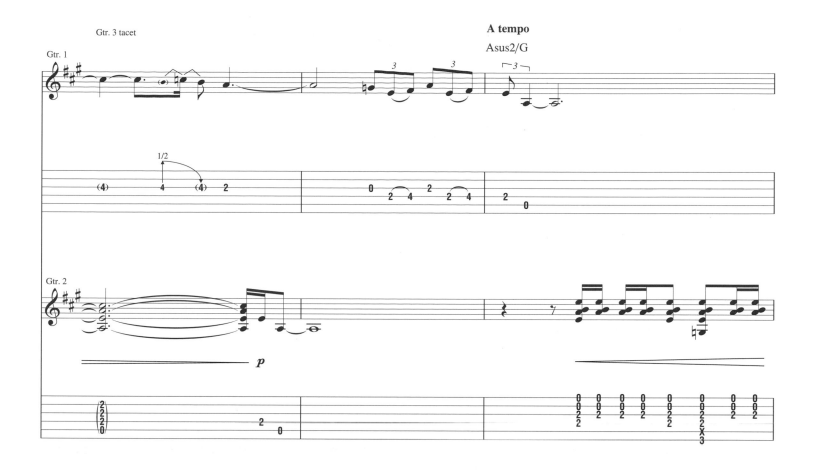

Come to My Window

Words and Music by Melissa Etheridge

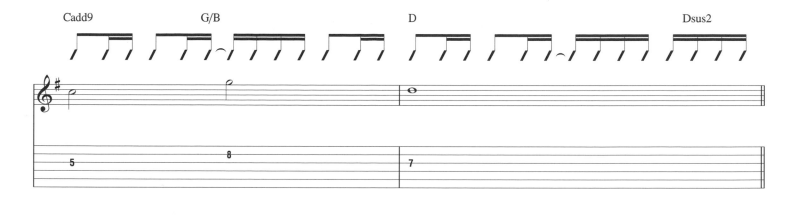

Verse

Gtr. 1 tacet
Gtr. 2: w/ Rhy. Fig. 1 (2 times)

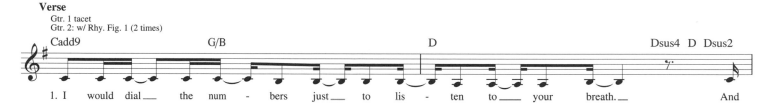

1. I would dial ___ the num - bers just ___ to lis - ten to ___ your breath. ___ And

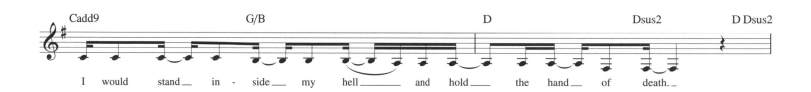

I would stand ___ in - side ___ my hell ___ and hold ___ the hand ___ of death. ___

You don't know ___ how far ___ I'd go ___ to case this ___ pre - cious ache. ___ And

you don't know ___ how much ___ I'd give ___ or how much I ___ can take. ___ Just to reach

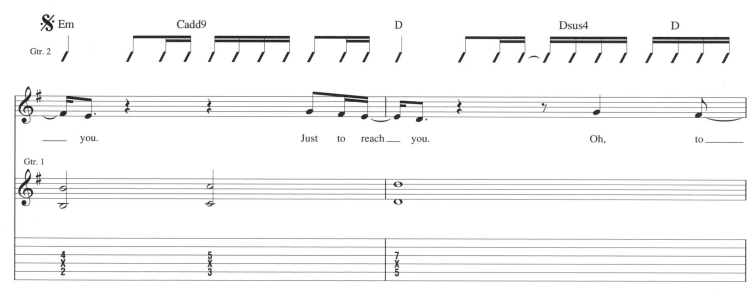

___ you. Just to reach ___ you. Oh, to ___

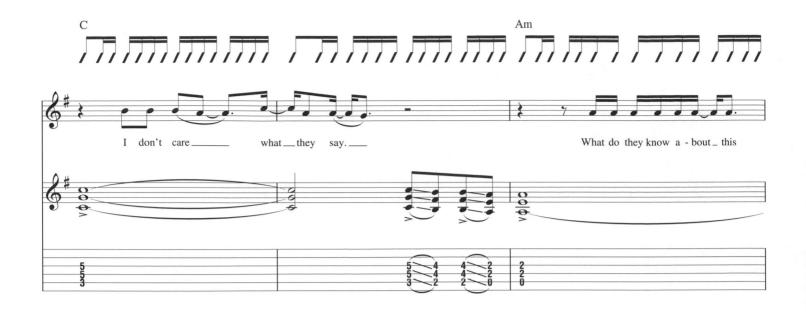

I don't care_____ what__ they say._____ What do they know a - bout__ this

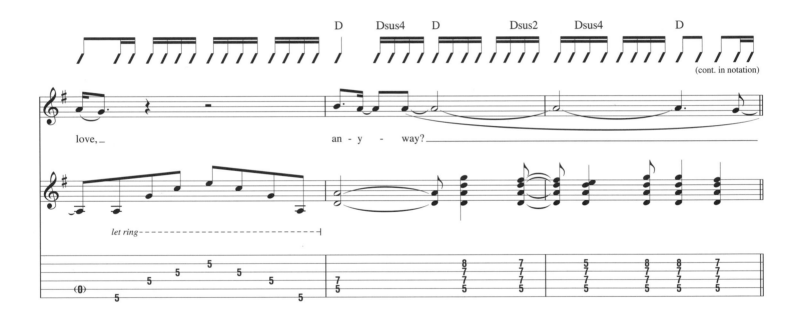

love,__ an - y - way?_____

(cont. in notation)

let ring - - - - - - - - - - - - - - - - - - -

Interlude

Gtr. 1 tacet

G   Cadd9   A7sus4   Dsus4   D Dsus2   D Dsus2

Gtr. 2

let ring -

Crazy Little Thing Called Love

Words and Music by Freddie Mercury

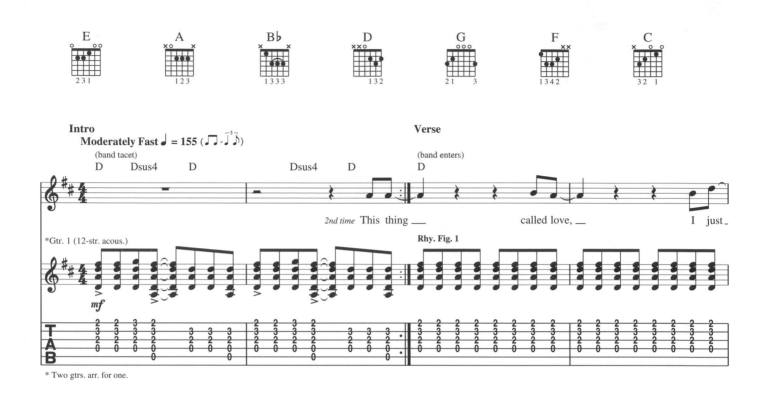

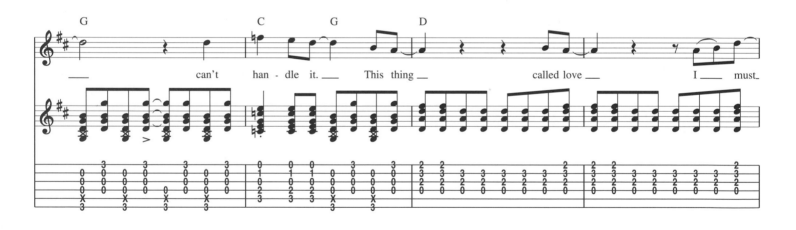

take a long ride on my mo-tor-bike ___ un-til I'm read-y. ___ Cra-zy lit-tle thing called love. __

Guitar Solo

(cont. in notation)

Yeah.

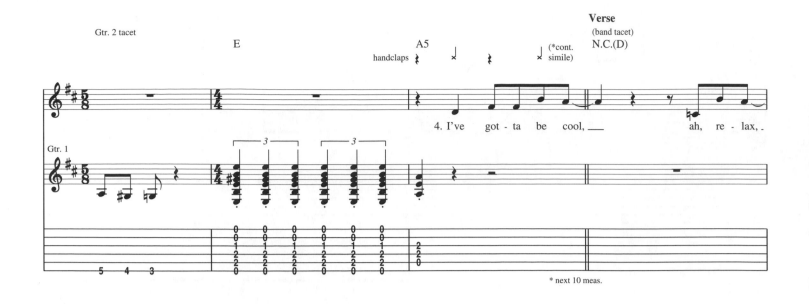

4. I've got ta be cool, __ ah, re - lax, __

get hip, __ and get on __ my tracks. __ Take a back - seat, hitch - hike, __

(Ah, mm. Ah,

and take a long ride on my mo - tor - bike __ un - til I'm read - y.

mm. Mm. __ I'm read - y, Fred - die.)

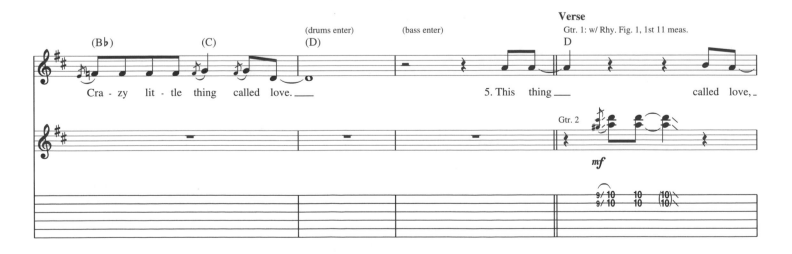

Cra - zy lit - tle thing called love. __

5. This thing __ called love, __

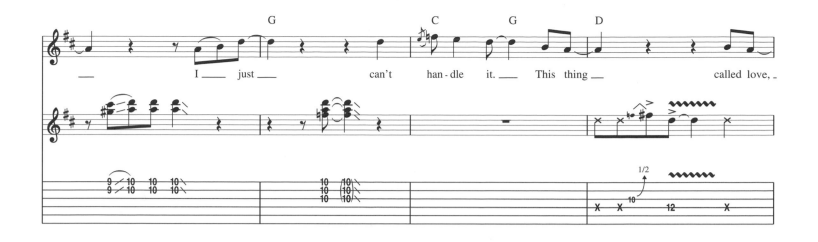

I — just — can't han-dle it. — This thing — called love, —

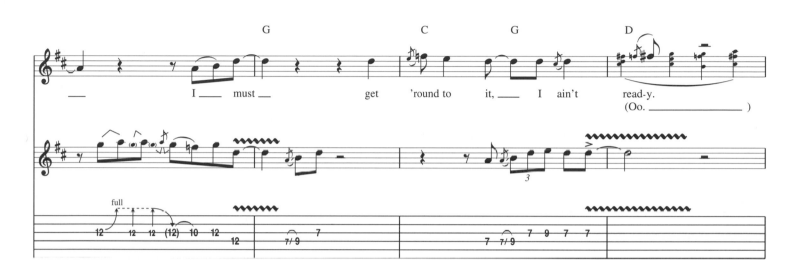

I — must — get 'round to it, — I ain't read-y.
(Oo. _____)

Outro-Chorus

Bb   C   D   Bb   C   D

w/ Bkdg. Voc. Fig. 1, till end

Rhy. Fig. 2   End Rhy. Fig. 2
Gtr. 1

Cra-zy lit-tle thing called love. —   Cra-zy lit-tle thing called love. —

Bkgd. Voc. Fig. 1

(Yeah, yeah.)

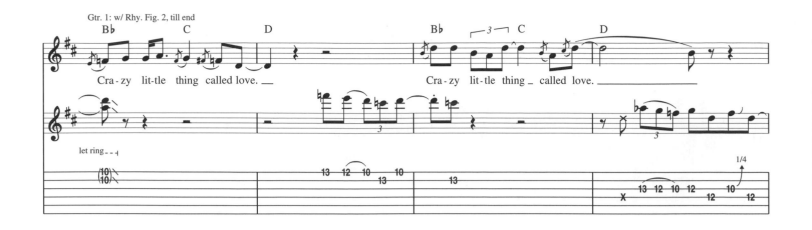

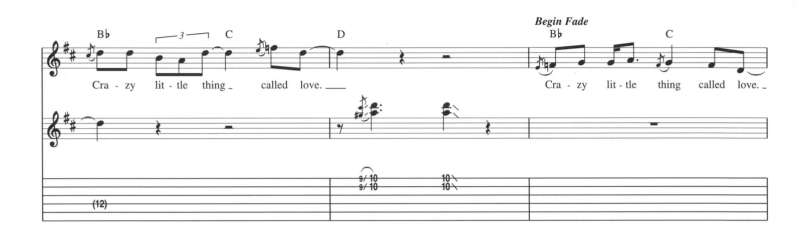

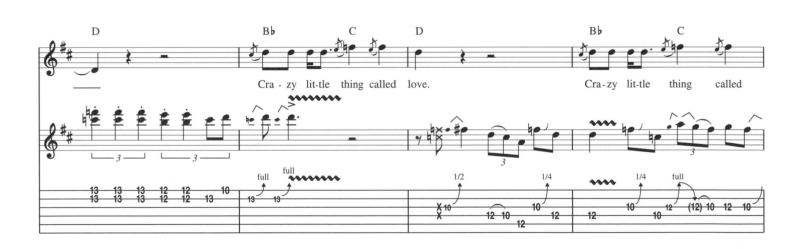

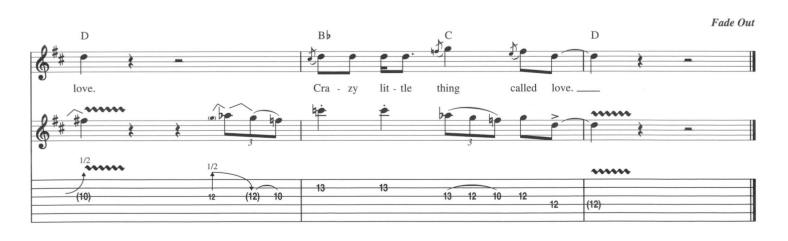

Drive

Words and Music by Brandon Boyd, Michael Einziger, Alex Katunich, Jose Pasillas II and Chris Kilmore

Pre-Chorus

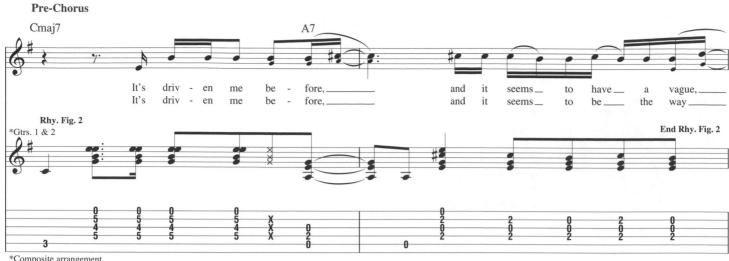

It's driv - en me be - fore,_____ and it seems_ to have_ a vague,_
It's driv - en me be - fore,_____ and it seems_ to be_ the way_

Rhy. Fig. 2

*Gtrs. 1 & 2

End Rhy. Fig. 2

*Composite arrangement

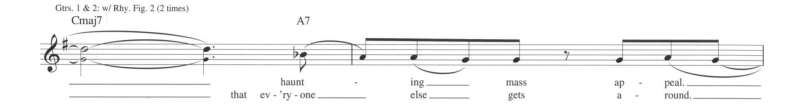

Gtrs. 1 & 2: w/ Rhy. Fig. 2 (2 times)

_____ haunt - ing_____ mass ap - peal._____
_____ that ev - 'ry - one_____ else_____ gets a - round._____

_____ But late - ly I'm_____ be - gin - ning to find_ that I_____
_____ But late - ly I'm_____ be - gin - ning to find_ that when_____

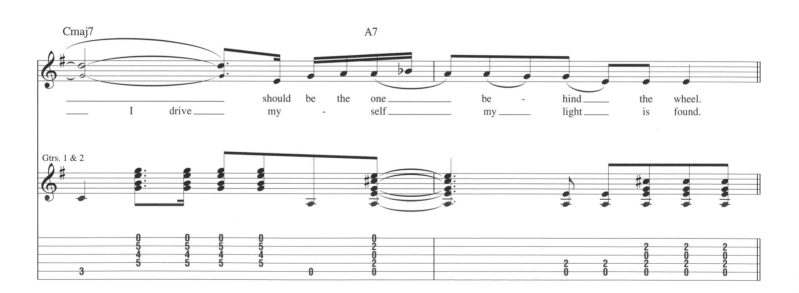

_____ should be the one_____ be - hind_ the wheel.
_____ I drive_ my - self_____ my light_ is found.

Gtrs. 1 & 2

Chorus

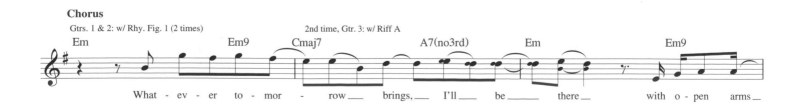

Gtrs. 1 & 2: w/ Rhy. Fig. 1 (2 times)

2nd time, Gtr. 3: w/ Riff A

What - ev - er to - mor - row brings,_ I'll be_ there_ with o - pen arms_

62

there _with o-pen arms_ _and o-pen eyes,_ _yeah._ What-ev-er to-mor-

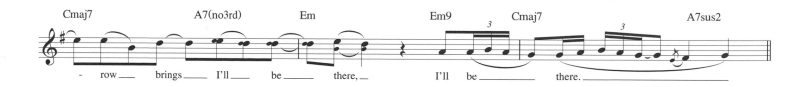

-row _brings_ I'll be _there,_ I'll be _there._

Outro

Gtrs. 1 & 2: w/ Rhy. Fig. 1 (2 times)
Gtr. 3: w/ Riff C (3 times)

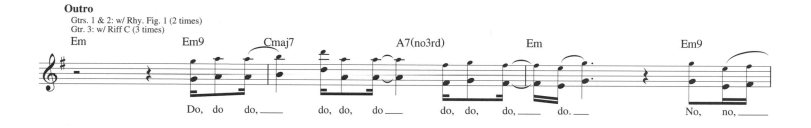

Do, do do, _do, do, do_ _do, do, do, do._ No, no,

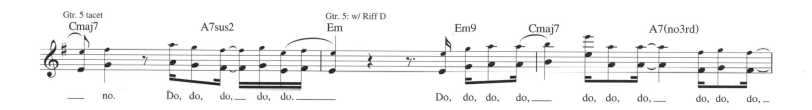

_no._ Do, do, do, _do, do._ Do, do, do, do, _do, do, do,_ _do, do, do,_

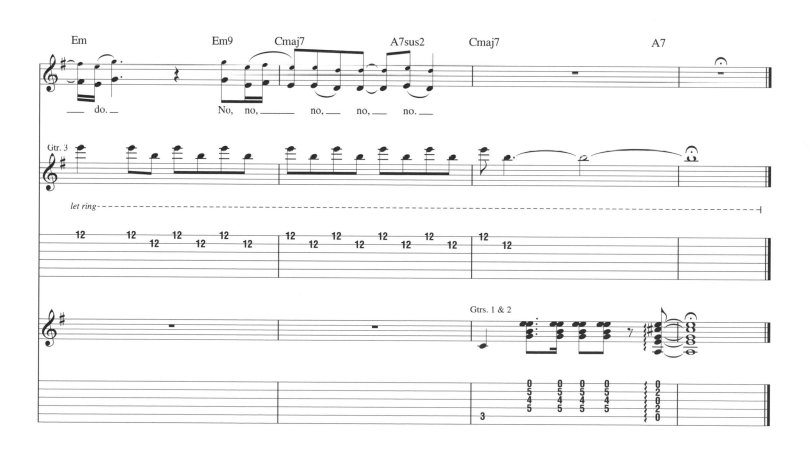

_do._ No, no, _no,_ no, _no._

Free Fallin'

Words and Music by Tom Petty and Jeff Lynne

Capo I

Intro
Moderately Slow ♩ = 84
drums tacet

*Symbols in parentheses represent chord names respective to capoed guitar.
Symbols above reflect actual sounding chord. Capoed fret is "0" in TAB.

Verse

good girl, ___ loves her ma - ma, loves Je - sus, ___ and A -

mer - i - ca, __ too. __ She's a good girl, __ cra - zy 'bout El - vis, loves

hor - ses __ and her boy - friend, too. __

*% Gtrs. 1 & 2: w/ Rhy. Figs. 1 & 1A, 4 times, simile

Verse

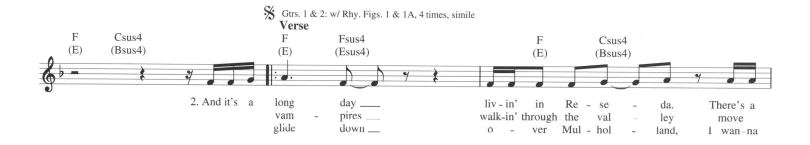

2. And it's a long day __ liv - in' in Re - se - da. There's a
vam - pires __ walk-in' through the val - ley move
glide down __ o - ver Mul - hol - land, I wan - na

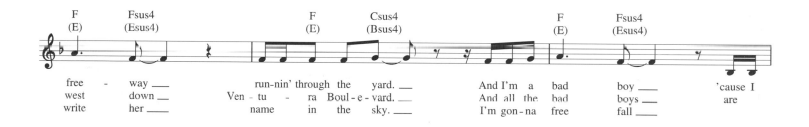

free - way __ run-nin' through the yard. __ And I'm a bad boy __ 'cause I
west down __ Ven - tu - ra Boul-e-vard. __ And all the bad boys __ are
write her __ name in the sky. __ I'm gon-na free fall __ out

To Coda ⊕

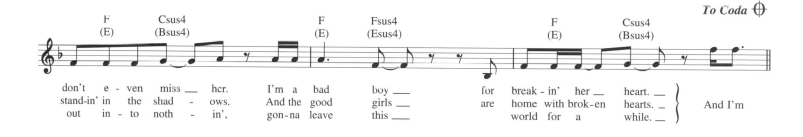

don't e - ven miss __ her. I'm a bad boy __ for break - in' her __ heart. __ } And I'm
stand-in' in the shad - ows. And the good girls __ are home with brok-en hearts. __
out in - to noth - in', gon-na leave this __ world for a while. __

Chorus
Gtrs. 1 & 2: w/ Rhy. Figs. 1 & 1A, 4 times, simile

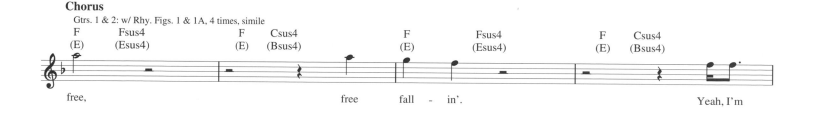

free, free fall - in'. Yeah, I'm

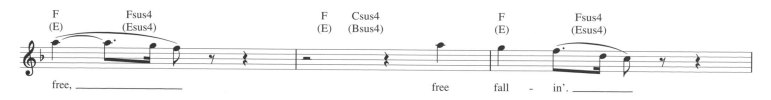

free, __ free fall - in'.

Give a Little Bit

Words and Music by Rick Davies and Roger Hodgson

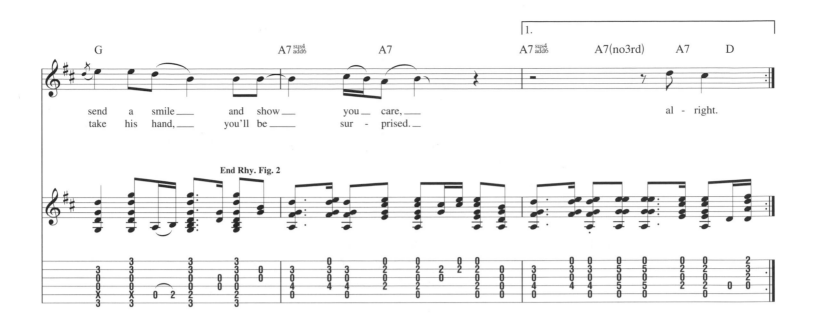

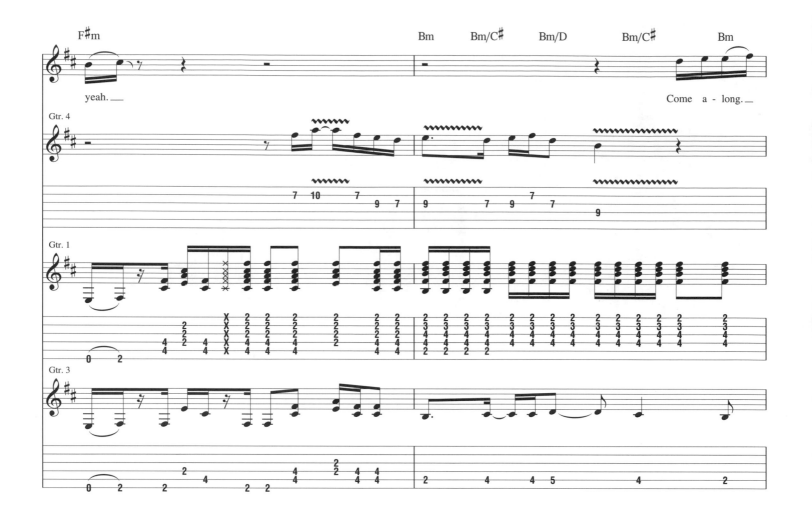

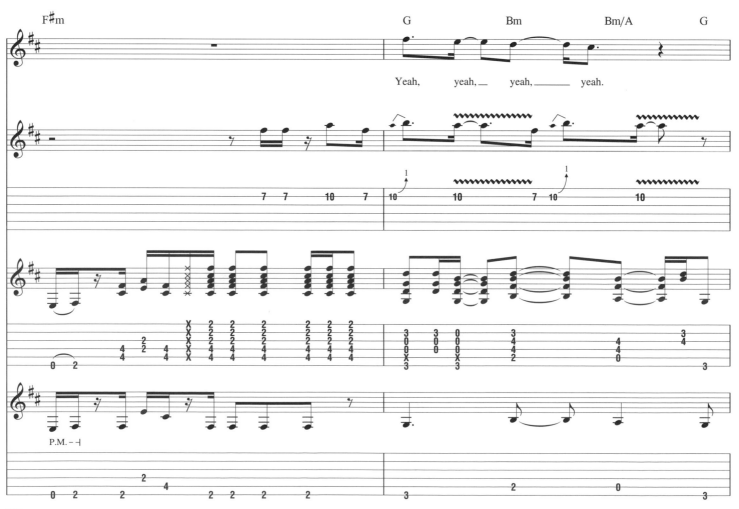

I'll give a lit - tle bit,_____ I'll give a lit - tle bit_____ of my life_____ for you.

Bridge

Now's the time_____ that we need_____ to share._____ So

find_____ your - self,_____ we're on_____ our way_____ back home. Oh, go - in' home,_____

_____ don't you need, don't you need to feel_____ at home?_____

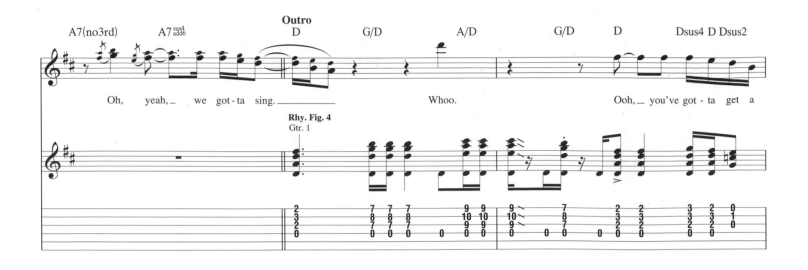

Oh, yeah,— we got-ta sing.— Whoo. Ooh,— you've got-ta get a

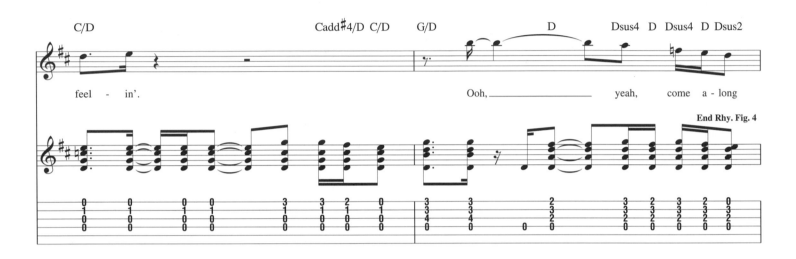

feel - in'. Ooh,————— yeah, come a - long

too.— Whoo. Yeah, come a - long too.—

Come a, come a, come a, oh, come a - long.

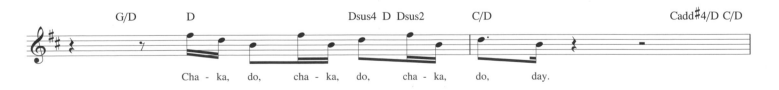

Cha - ka, do, cha - ka, do, cha - ka, do, day.

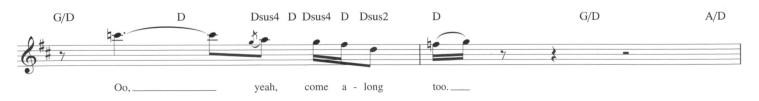

Oo,————— yeah, come a - long too.—

Have You Ever Really Loved a Woman?

Words and Music by Bryan Adams, Michael Kamen and Robert John Lange

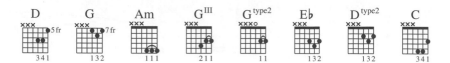

Gtr. 1: Drop D tuning:
(low to high) D–A–D–G–B–E

Intro

Slowly ♪ = 132

*Chord symbols reflect overall harmony.

*Two gtrs. arr. for one.

tell her that she's real-ly want-ed.   When

(cont. in slashes)

P.M.

you love a wom-an you tell her that she's _____ the one. _____

rake

'Cause she needs ___ some-bod - y   to tell her that   it's   gon - na last ___

for - ev - er.   So tell me have you ev - er   real - ly,

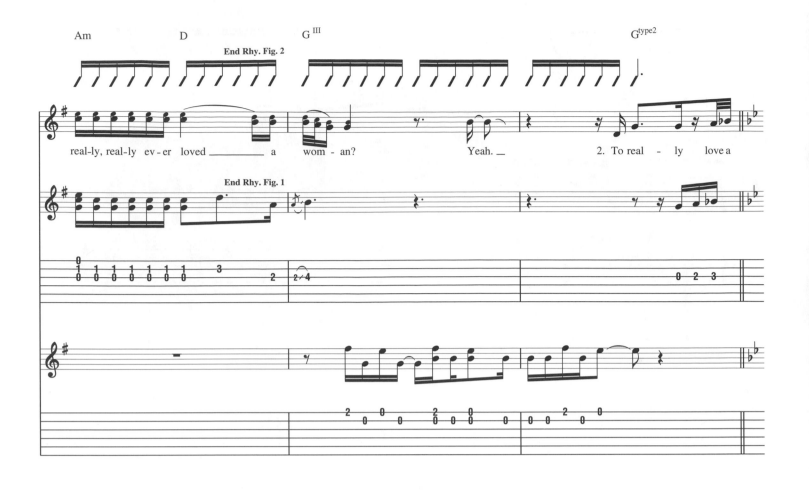

she needs ___ some-bod - y to tell her that you'll al - ways be _____ to - geth -

- er. So tell me have you ev - er real - ly, real - ly, real - ly ev - er loved ___ a

wom - an? ___ Oh, ___ you've got to give her some faith,

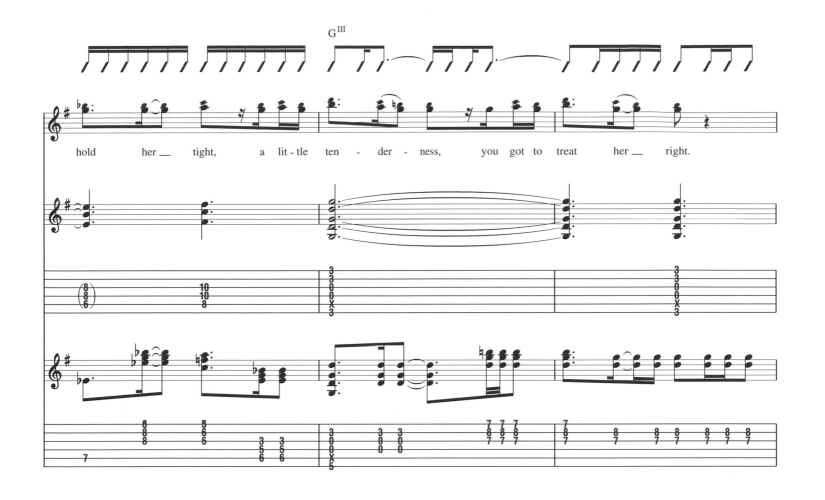

hold her __ tight, a lit-tle ten - der - ness, you got to treat her __ right.

She will be there for you tak - ing good care of you. __ You real-ly got to love __

(cont. in notation)

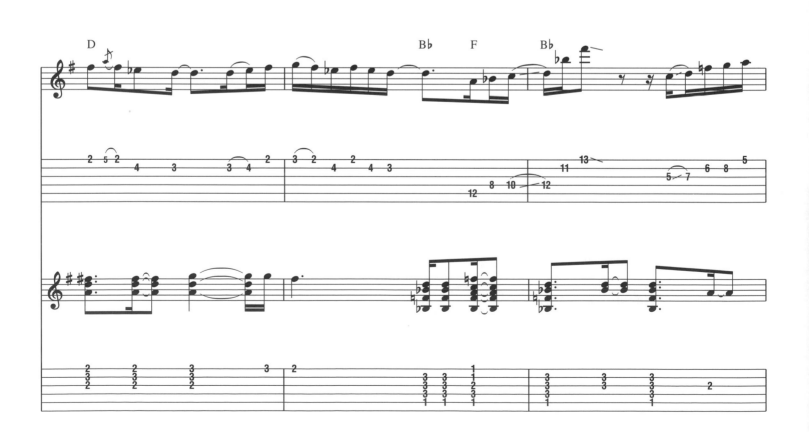

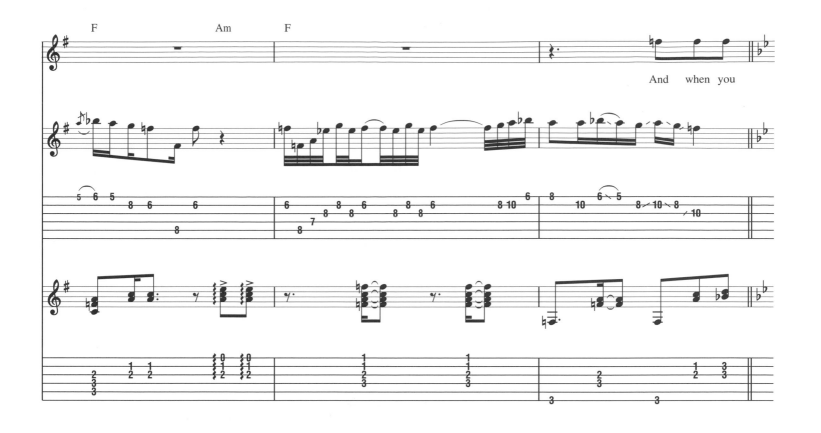

And when you

Interlude

Gtr. 3 tacet

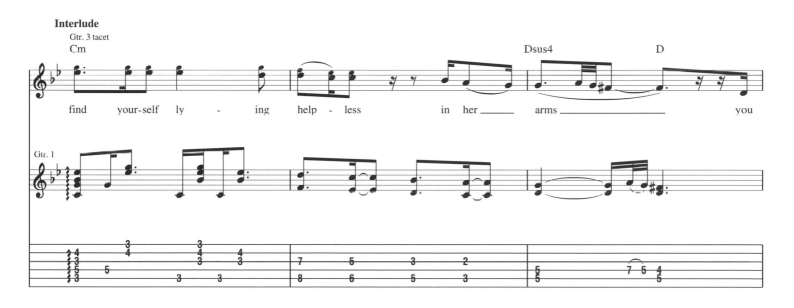

find your-self ly — ing help - less in her ____ arms _____ you

know you real - ly love _____ a wom - an. When

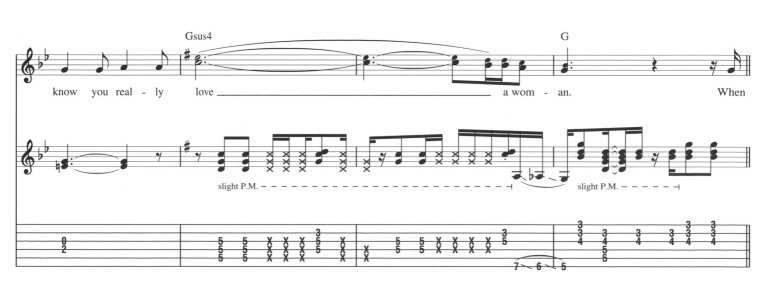

Gtr. 1: w/ Rhy. Fig. 1 (last 14 meas.)
Gtr. 3: w/ Rhy. Fig. 2 (last 14 meas.)

you love ___ a wom - an you tell her that she's ___ real - ly want - ed.

Gtr. 2

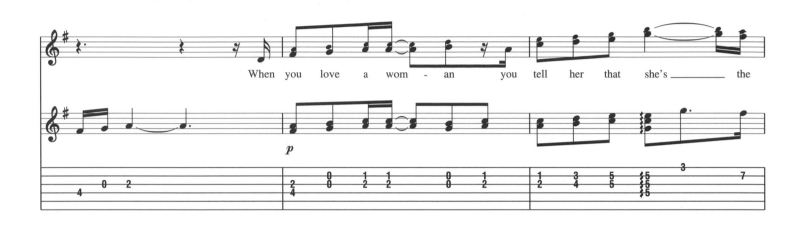

When you love a wom - an you tell her that she's _____ the

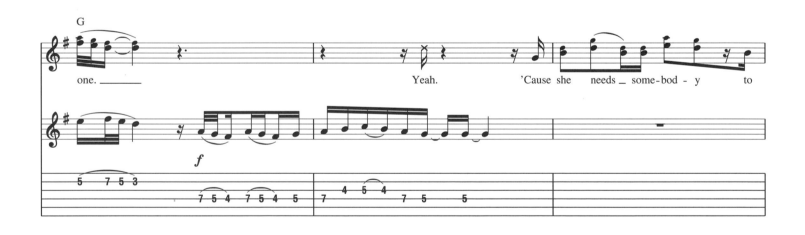

one. _____ Yeah. 'Cause she needs ___ some-bod - y to

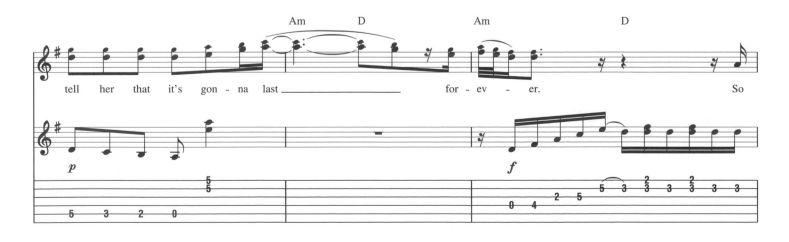

tell her that it's gon - na last _____ for - ev - er. So

Gtr. 2 tacet

tell me have you ev - er real - ly, real - ly, real - ly ev - er loved _____ a

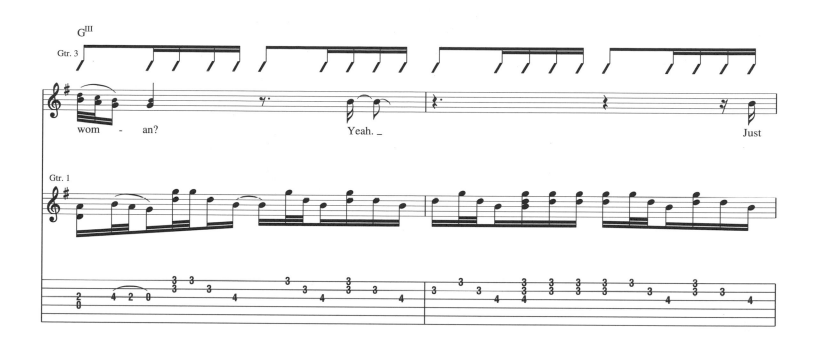

wom - an?   Yeah. _   Just

tell me have you ev - er real - ly, real - ly, real - ly ev - er loved _____ a wom - an?

Holiday

Words and Music by Klaus Meine and Rudolf Schenker

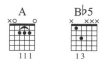

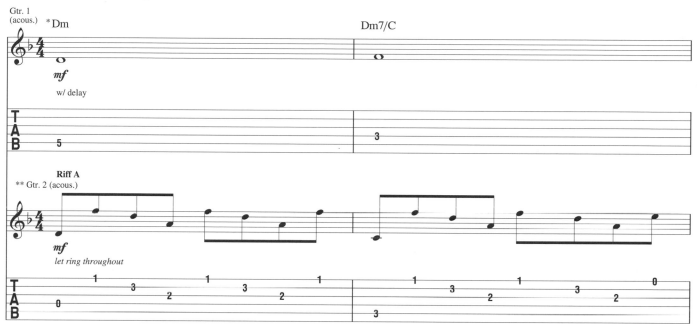

* Chord symbols reflect implied harmony.

** Doubled throughout

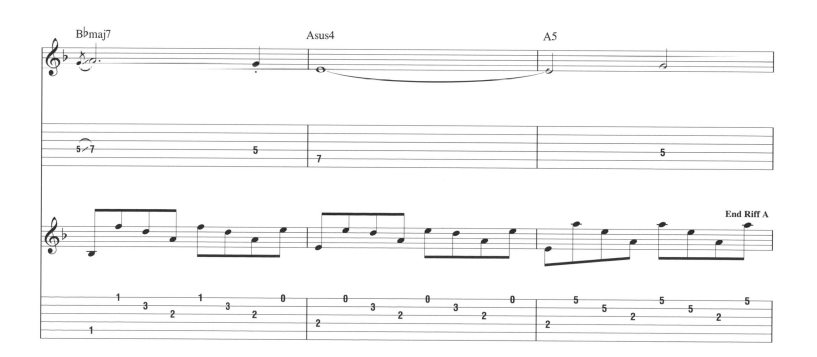

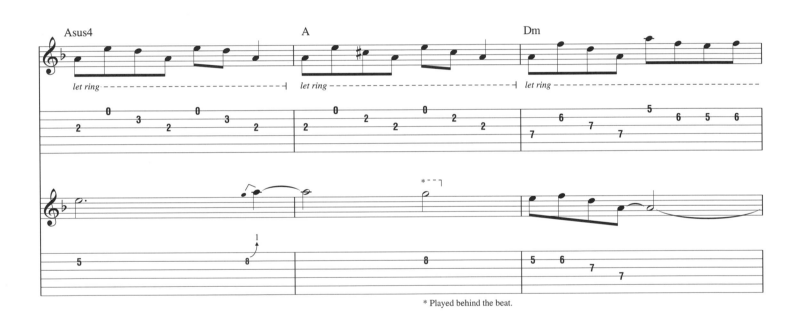

* Played behind the beat.

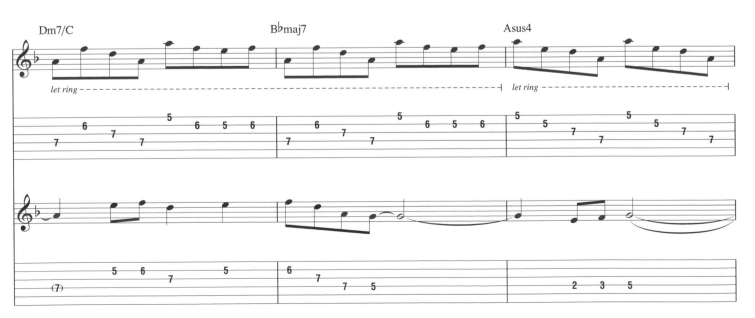

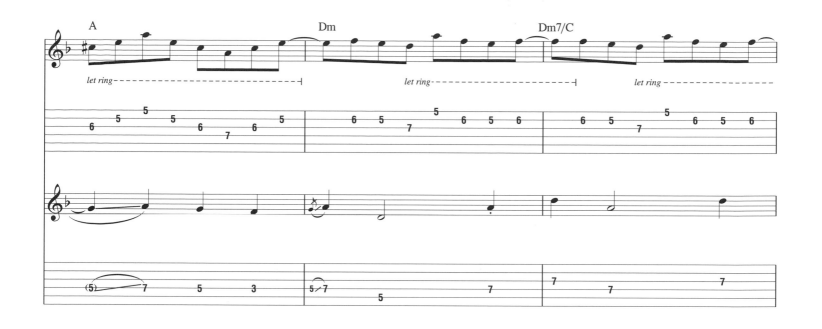

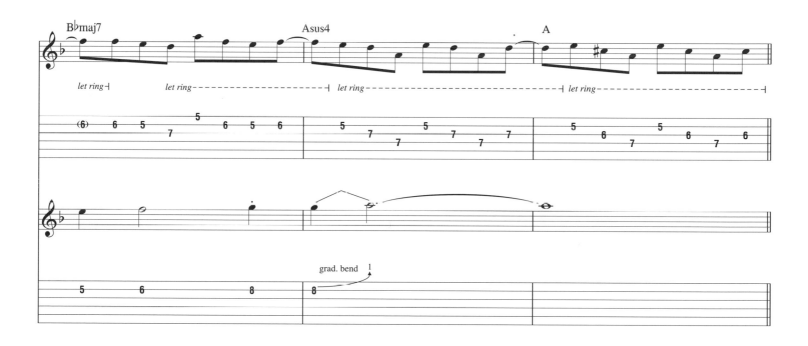

Verse

Gtrs. 1 & 3 tacet

1. Let me take you far a - way, ___ you'd like a

Riff B

Gtr. 2

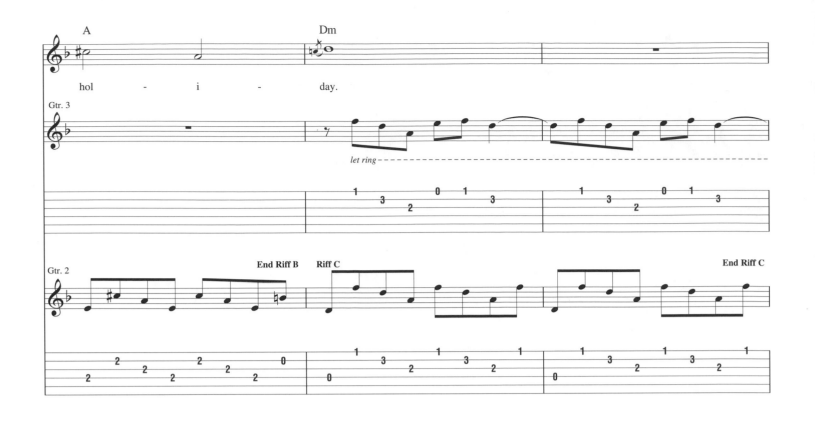

hol - i - day.

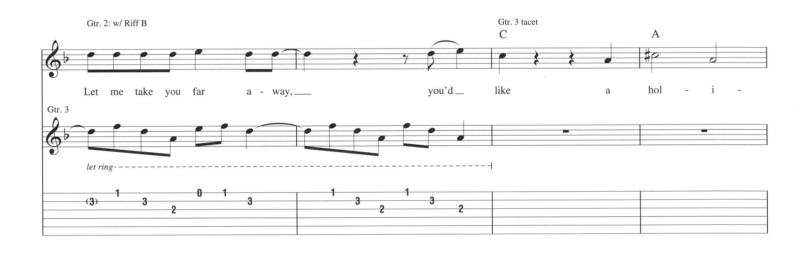

Let me take you far a - way, _____ you'd _____ like a hol - i -

day. Ex - change the cold days _____ for the

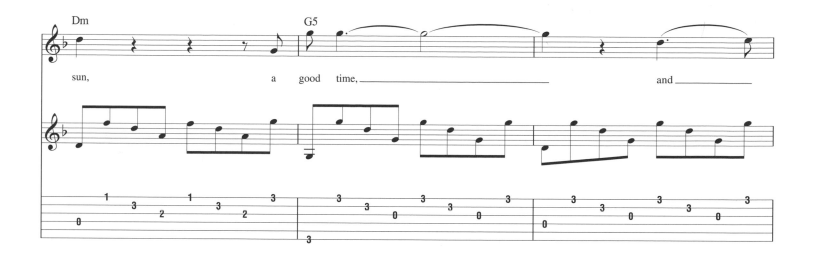

sun,   a good time,   and

Gtr. 2: w/ Riff B

fun.   Let me take you far a - way,

End Riff E

Gtr. 2: w/ Riff A (2 times)

  you'd like a hol - i - day.

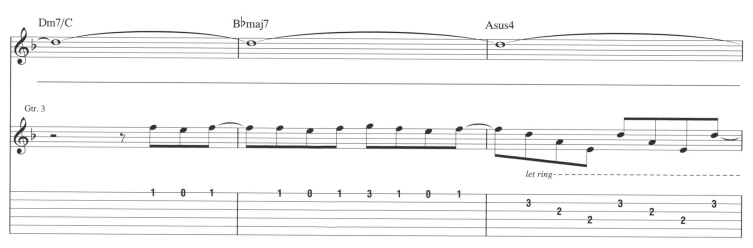

Gtr. 3

let ring- - - - - - - - - - - - - - - - - - - -

Interlude

Verse

Gtr. 2: w/ Riff B

2. Let me take you far a - way, _____ you'd like a

Gtr. 2: w/ Riff C

hol - i - day.

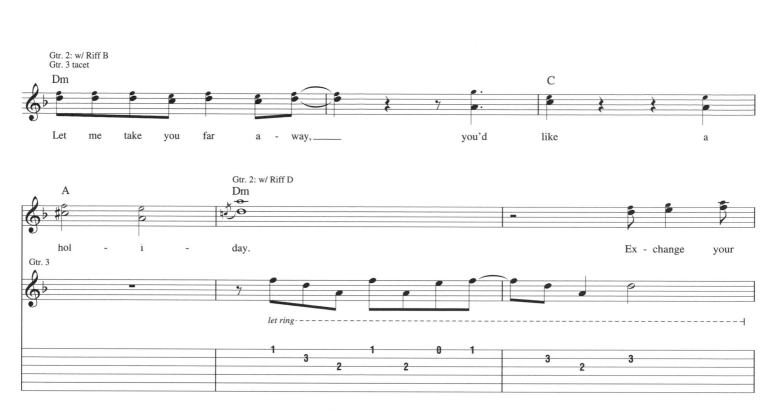

Let me take you far a - way, _____ you'd like a hol - i - day.

Gtr. 2: w/ Riff D

Ex - change your

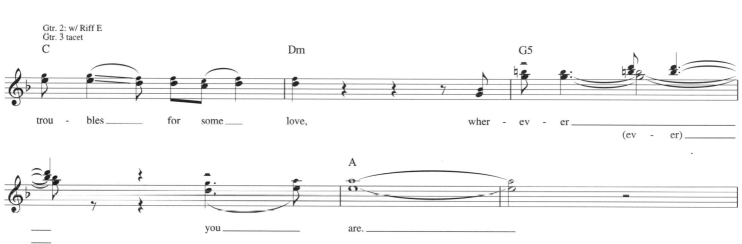

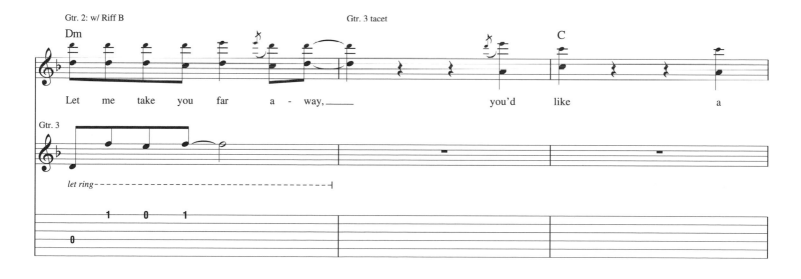

trou - bles _____ for some _____ love, wher - ev - er _____ (ev - er) _____ you _____ are. _____

Gtr. 2: w/ Riff B   Gtr. 3 tacet

Let me take you far a - way, _____ you'd like a

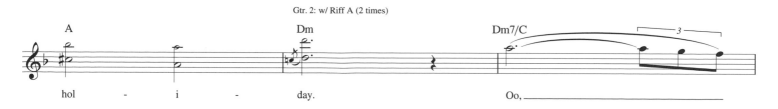

Gtr. 2: w/ Riff A (2 times)

hol - i - day.   Oo, _____

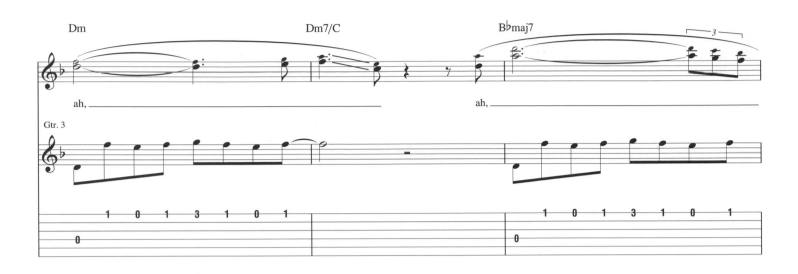

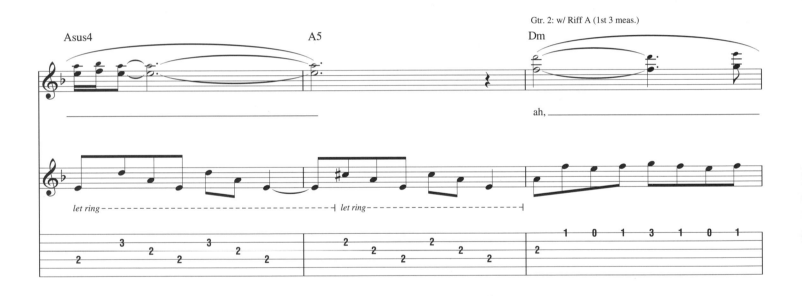

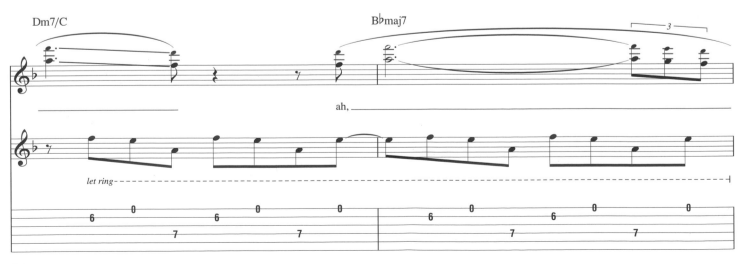

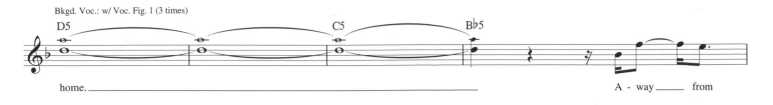

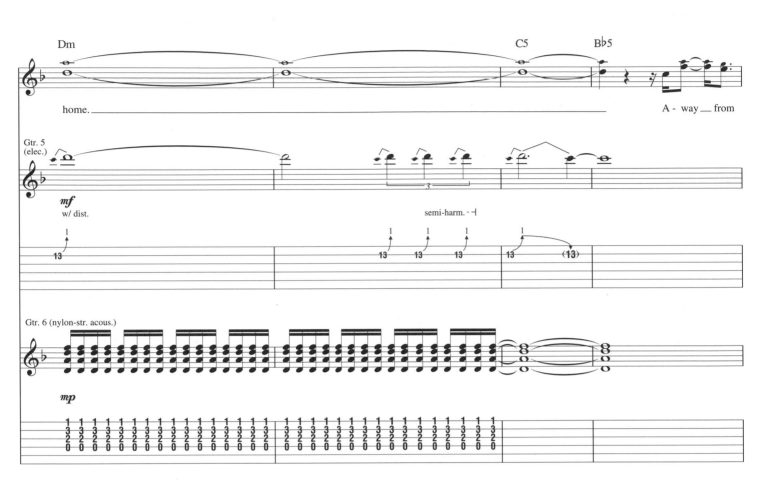

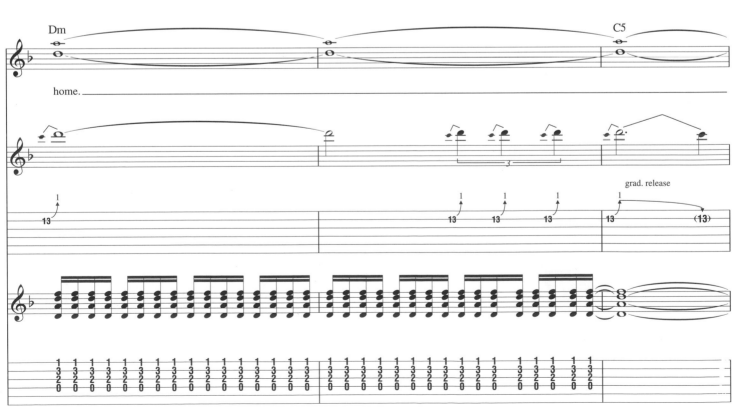

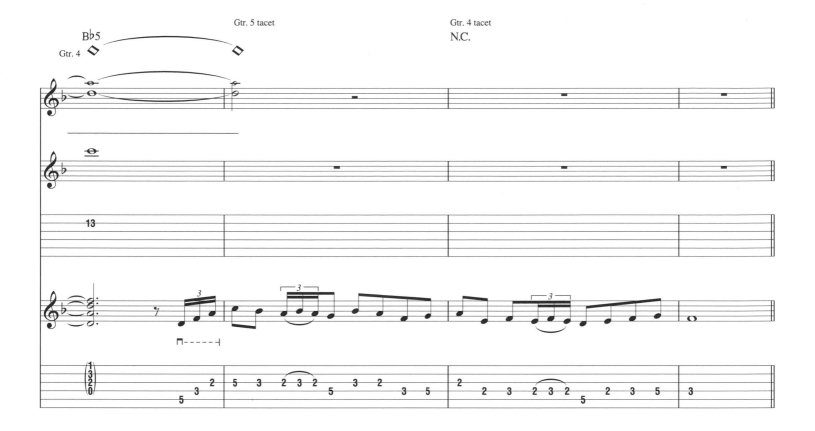

Outro-Guitar Solo

Gtr. 2: w/ Riff A (till fade)
Gtr. 6 tacet

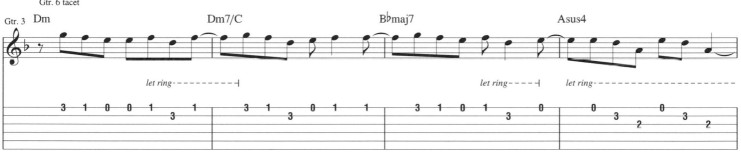

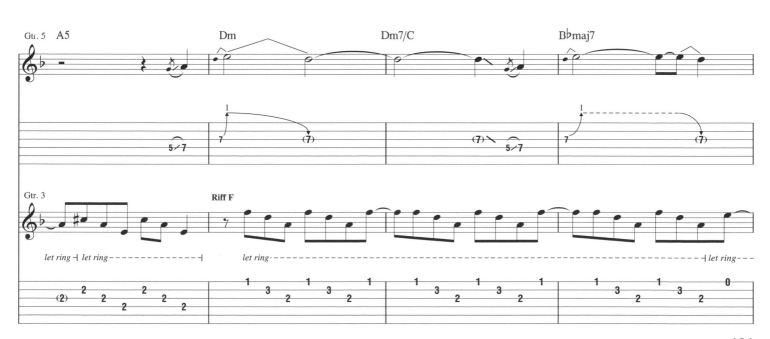

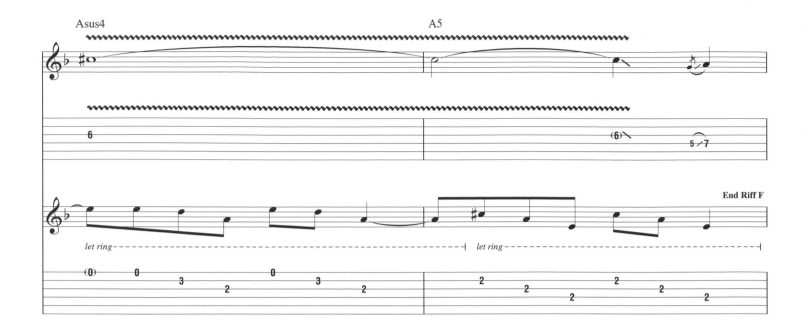

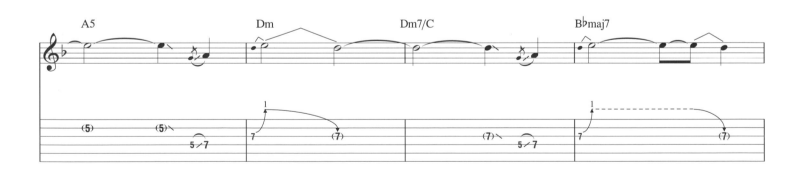

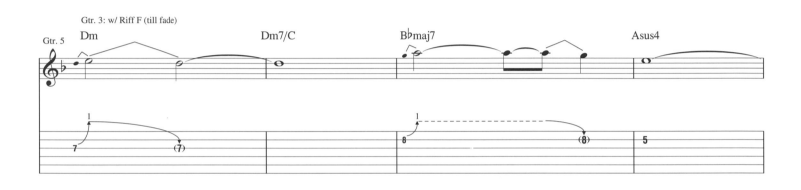

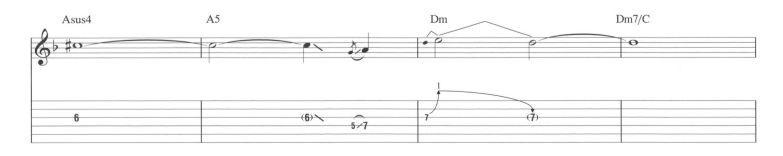

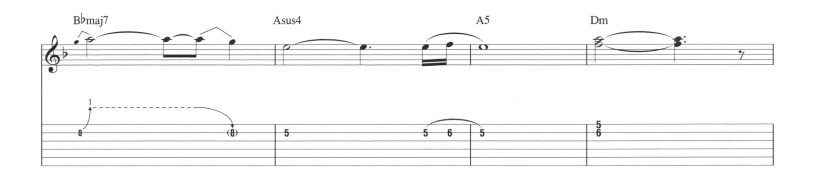

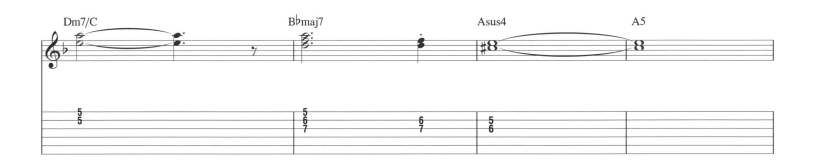

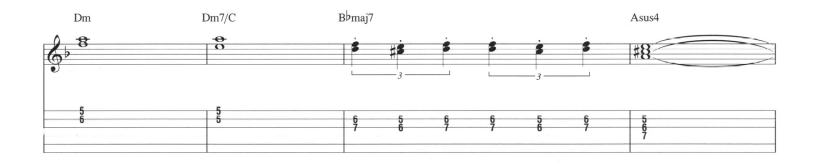

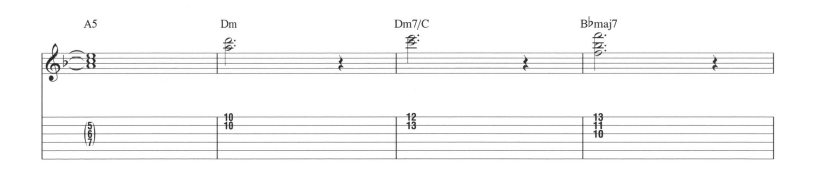

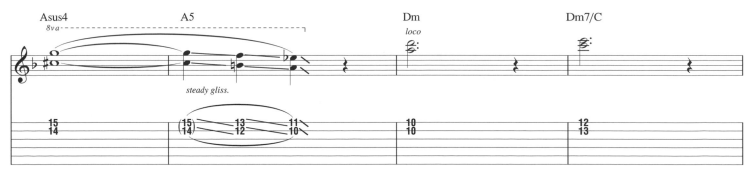

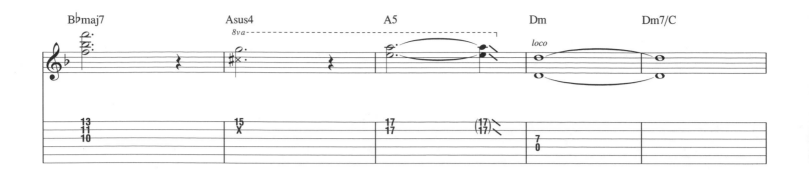

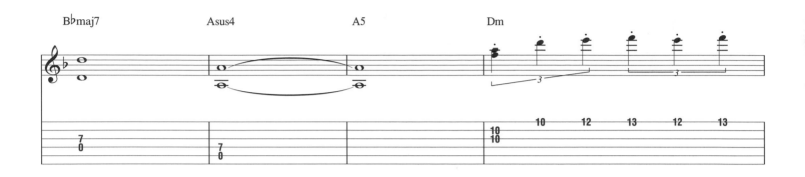

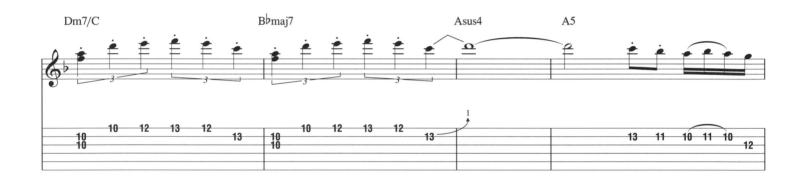

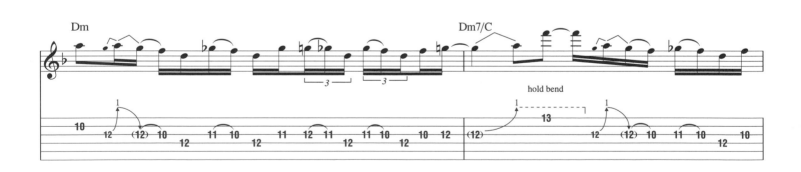

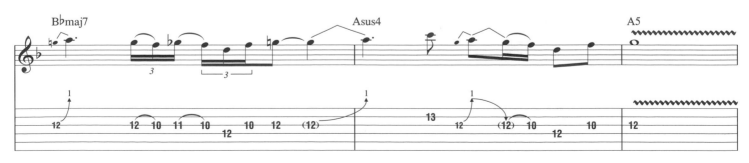

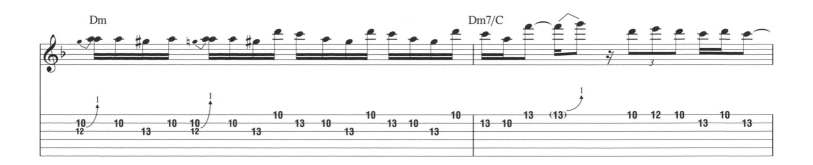

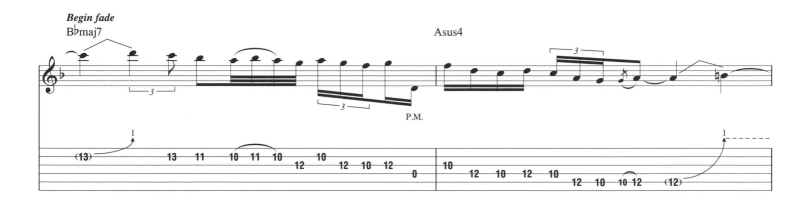

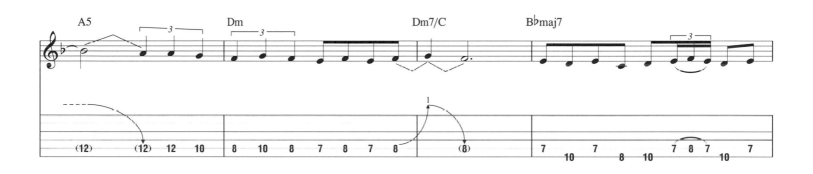

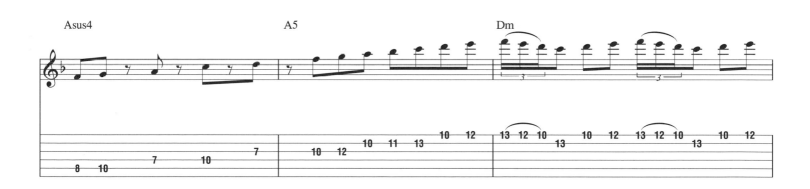

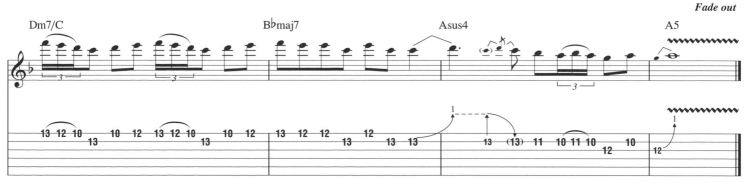

I Will

Words and Music by John Lennon and Paul McCartney

I'll Have to Say I Love You in a Song

Words and Music by Jim Croce

*Chord symbols reflect implied harmony.

**Symbols in parentheses represent chord names respective to capoed guitar.
Symbols above reflect actual sounding chords. Capoed fret is "0" in tab.

Verse
2nd time, Gtr. 2: w/ Fill 1

know it's kind of late, ___
know it's kind of strange ___

I hope I did-n't wake ___ you.
but ev-'ry time I'm near ___ you,

But what I
I just

Riff B1

Riff B

got - ta say ___ can't wait. ___
run out of things ___ to say. ___

I know you'd un-der - stand. ___

End Riff B1

End Riff B

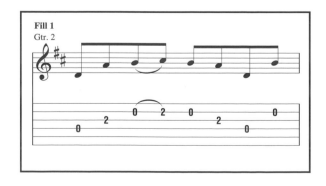

Fill 1
Gtr. 2

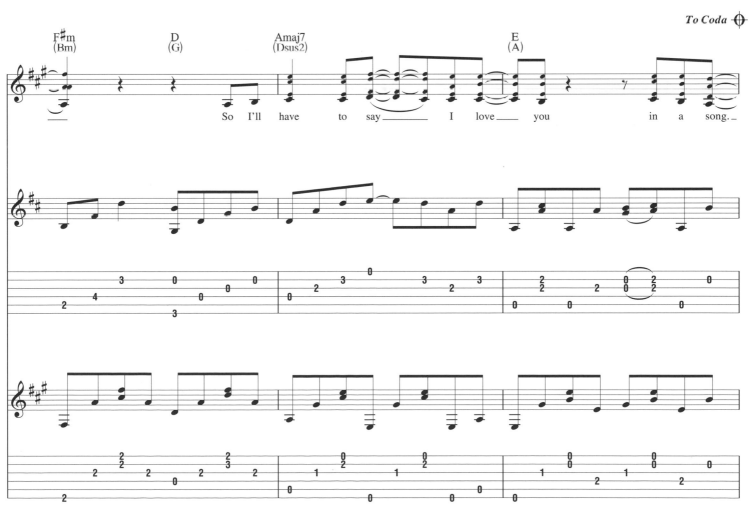

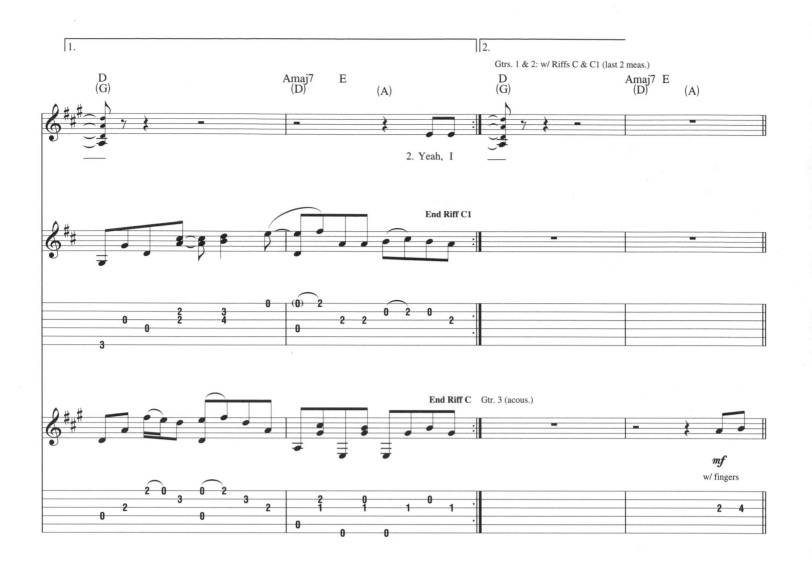

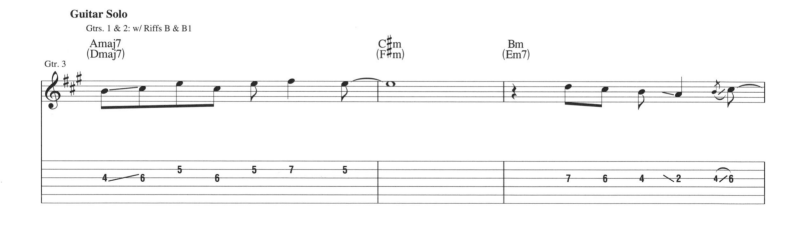

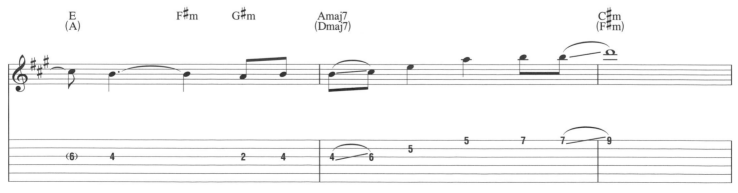

113

114

If You Could Only See

Words and Music by Emerson Hart

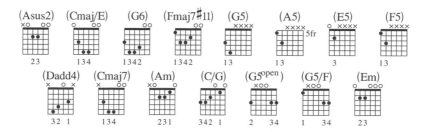

Capo I

Moderate Rock ♩ = 95

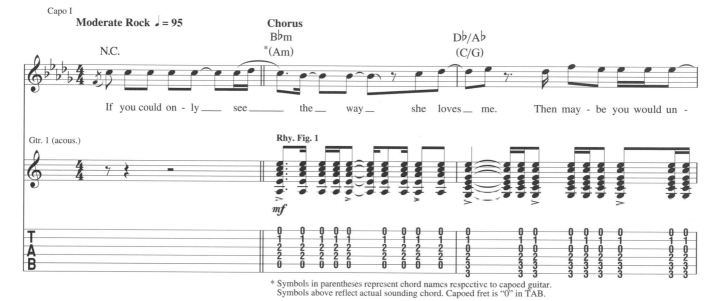

If you could on-ly see the way she loves me. Then may-be you would un-

* Symbols in parentheses represent chord names respective to capoed guitar.
Symbols above reflect actual sounding chord. Capoed fret is "0" in TAB.

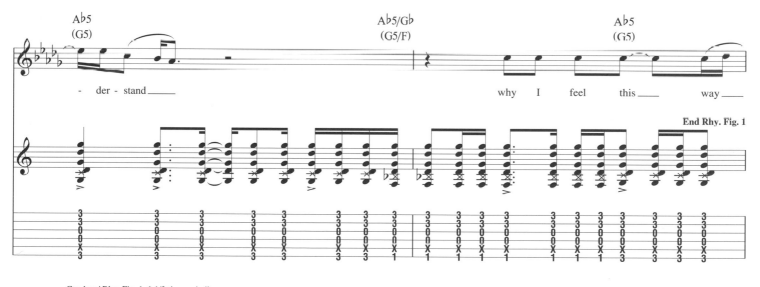

-der-stand why I feel this way

a-bout our love, and what I must do.

If you could on-ly see how blue her eyes can be when she says,

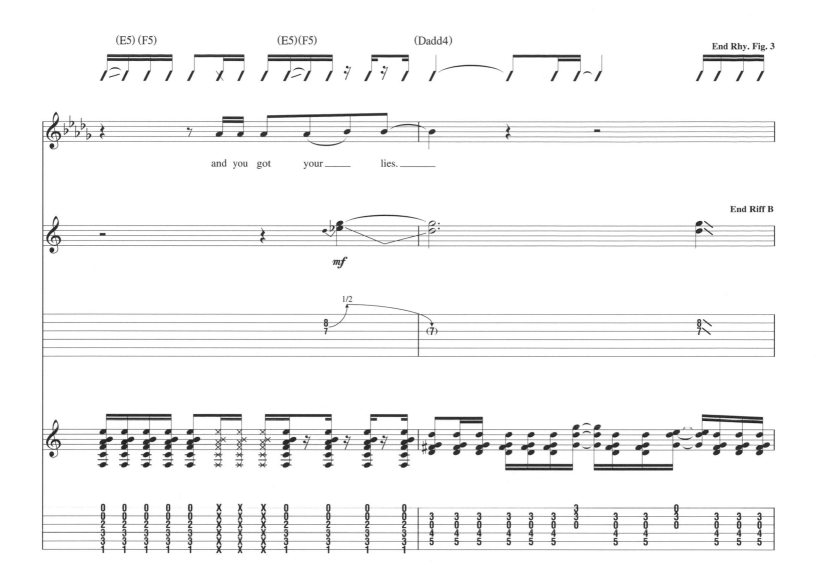

and you got your _____ lies. _____

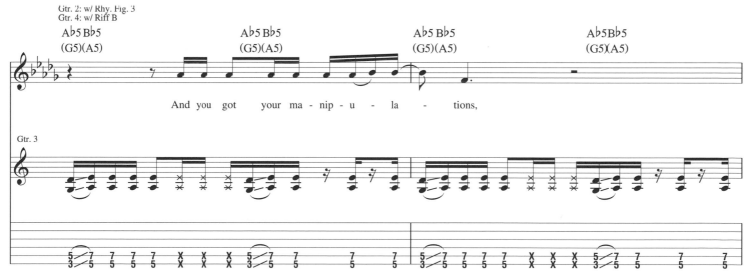

And you got your ma - nip - u - la - tions,

* Chord symbols reflect combined harmony.

119

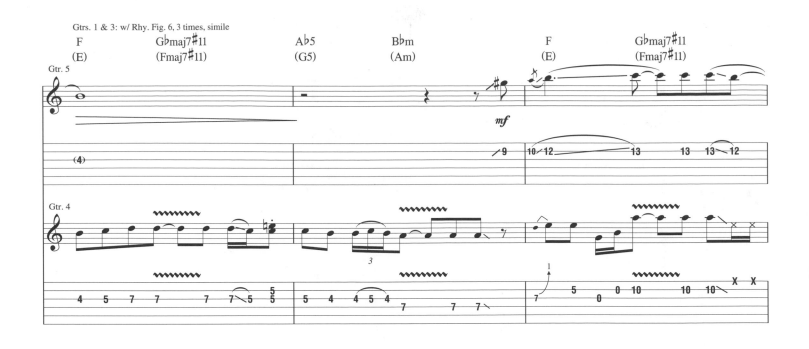

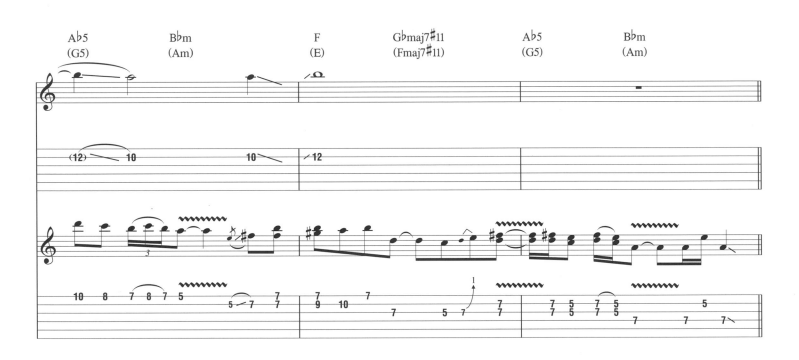

Pre-Chorus

Bkgd. Voc.: w/ Voc. Fig. 1
Gtr. 3: w/ Rhy. Fig. 5

Say-in' you love but you___ don't.___ You give your love but you___ won't.

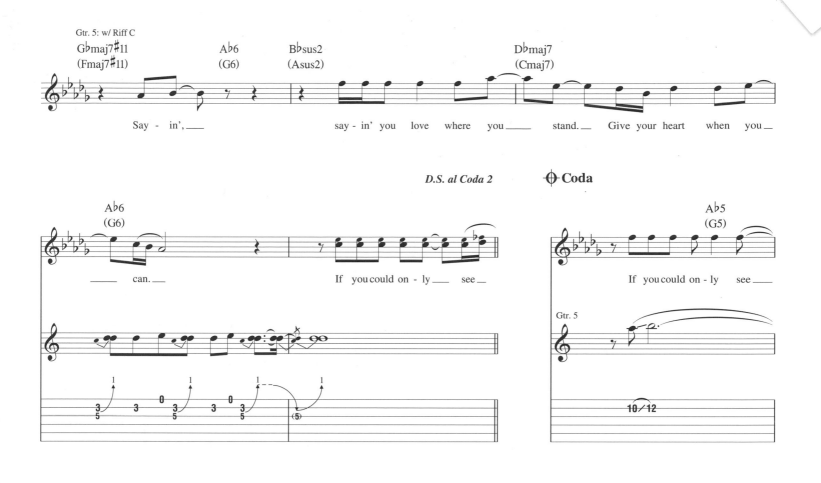

Gtr. 5: w/ Riff C

Gbmaj7#11 (Fmaj7#11) Ab6 (G6) Bbsus2 (Asus2) Dbmaj7 (Cmaj7)

Say - in', ___ say - in' you love where you ___ stand. Give your heart when you ___

D.S. al Coda 2 ⊕ **Coda**

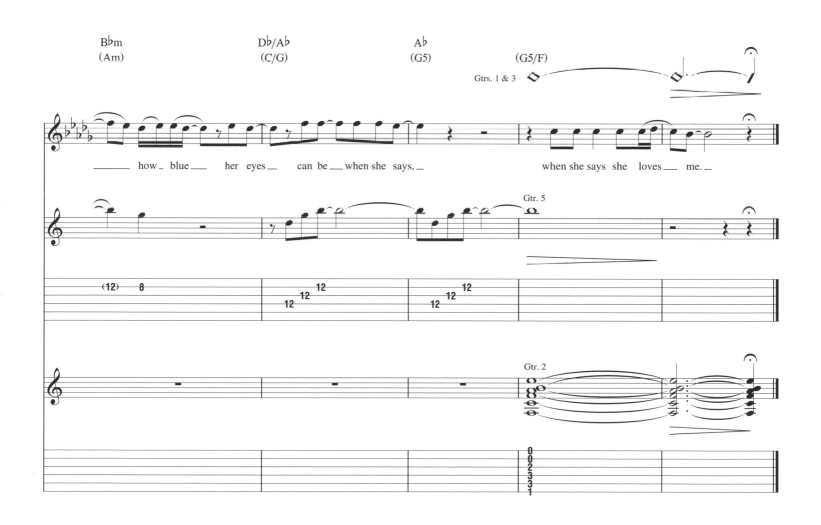

Ab6 (G6)

___ can. ___ If you could on - ly ___ see ___

Ab5 (G5)

If you could on - ly see ___

Gtr. 5

Bbm (Am) Db/Ab (C/G) Ab (G5) (G5/F)

___ how ___ blue ___ her eyes ___ can be ___ when she says, ___ when she says she loves ___ me.

Gtr. 5

Gtr. 2

Gtrs. 1 & 3

Jumper

Words and Music by Stephan Jenkins

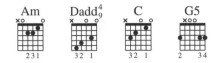

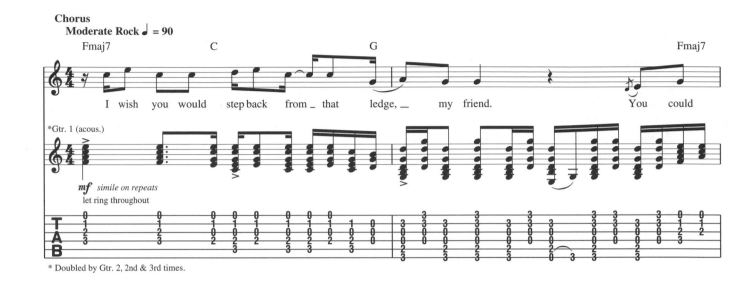

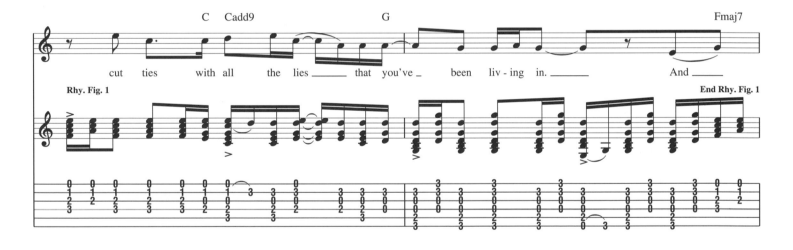

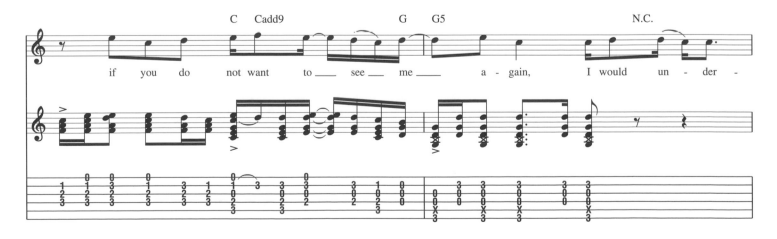

* Doubled by Gtr. 2, 2nd & 3rd times.

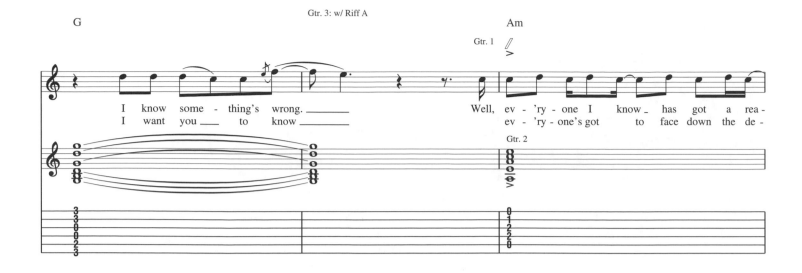

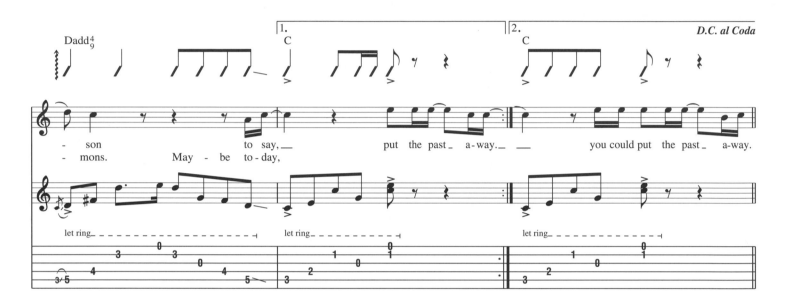

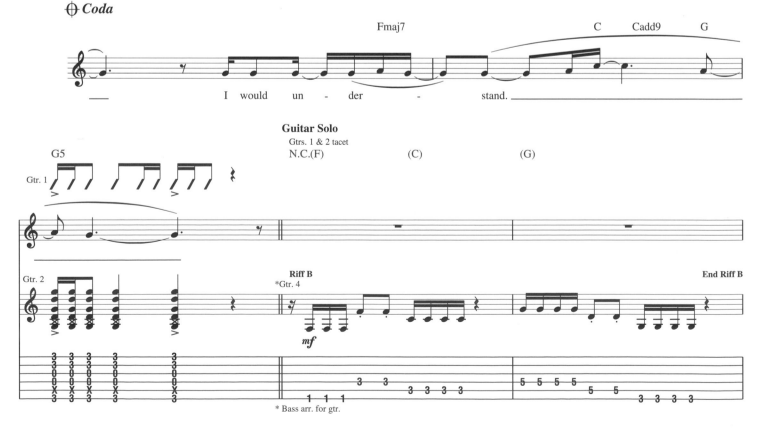

126

More Than Words

Words and Music by Nuno Bettencourt and Gary Cherone

Tune down 1/2 step:
(low to high) Eb-Ab-Db-Gb-Bb-Eb

Intro

Moderately slow ♩ = 96

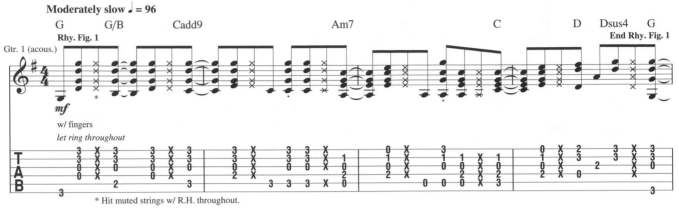

* Hit muted strings w/ R.H. throughout.

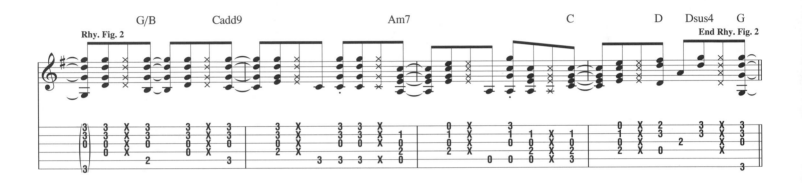

Verse

Gtr. 1: w/ Rhy. Fig. 2

1. Say - ing "I____ love____ you" is not the words___ I want___ to___ hear___ from you.___

____ It's not that I____ want____ you not to say,___ but if____

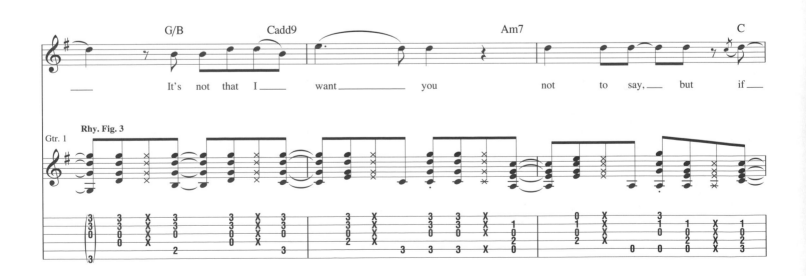

131

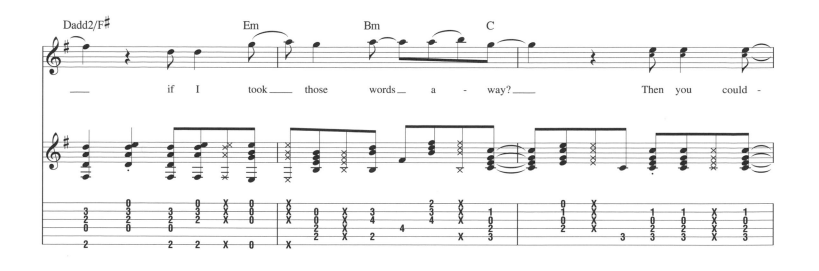

if I took___ those words___ a - way?___ Then you could -

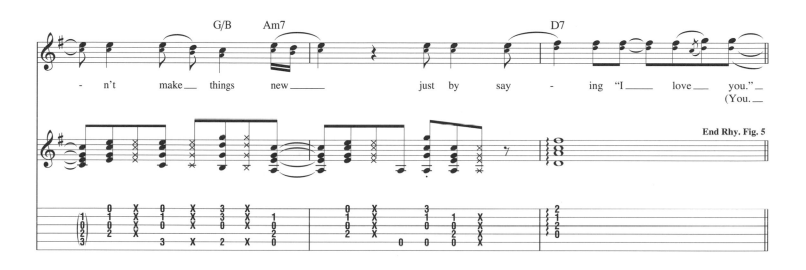

- n't make___ things new___ just by say - ing "I___ love___ you."___
(You.___

End Rhy. Fig. 5

Interlude

Gtr. 1: w/ Rhy. Fig. 1

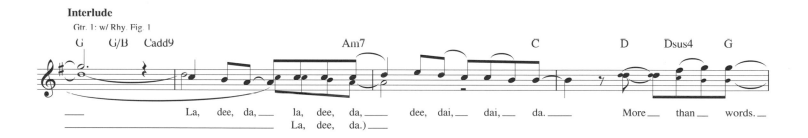

___ La, dee, da,___ la, dee, da,___ dee, dai,___ dai,___ da.___ More___ than___ words.___
La, dee, da.)___

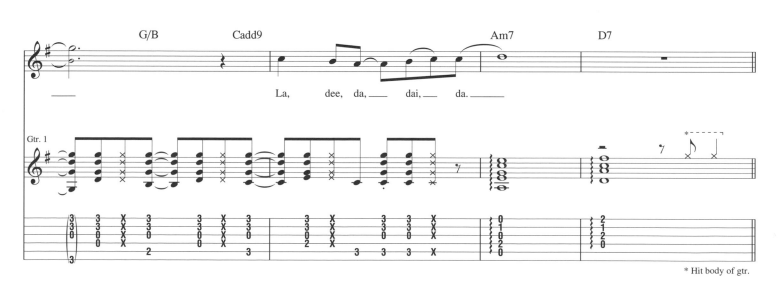

___ La, dee, da,___ dai,___ da.___

Gtr. 1

* Hit body of gtr.

Verse

Gtr. 1: w/ Rhy. Fig. 1

2. Now that I've tried to talk to you and make you un - der - stand,

Gtr. 1: w/ Rhy. Fig. 3

all you have to do is close your eyes and just

reach out your hands and touch me.

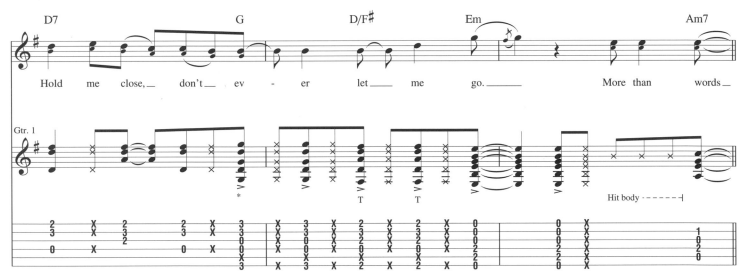

* Strum accented chords w/ nails (all downstrokes);
hit muted strings w/ R.H. as before.

Chorus

Gtr. 1: w/ Rhy. Fig. 4

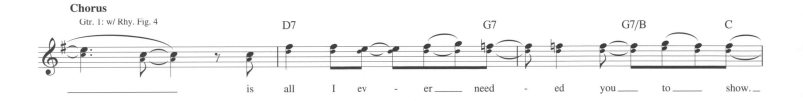

is all I ev - er need - ed you to show.

Then you would - n't have to say that you love me, 'cause

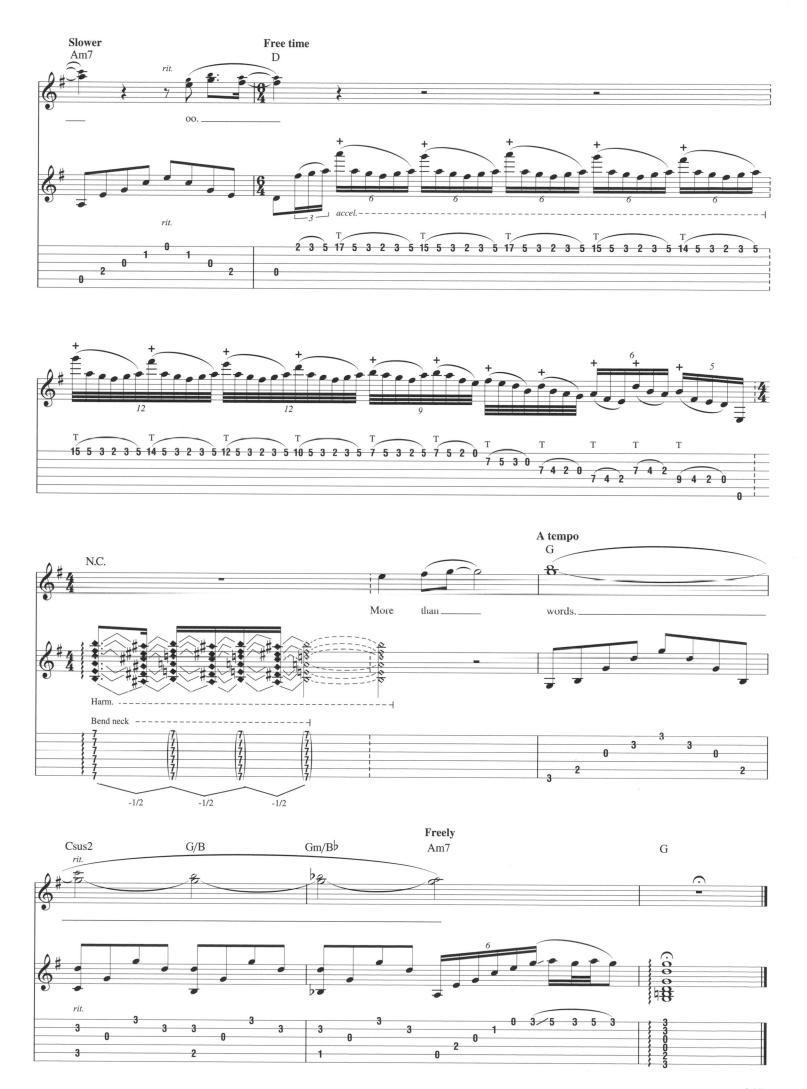

My Name Is Jonas

Words and Music by Rivers Cuomo, Jason Cropper and Patrick Wilson

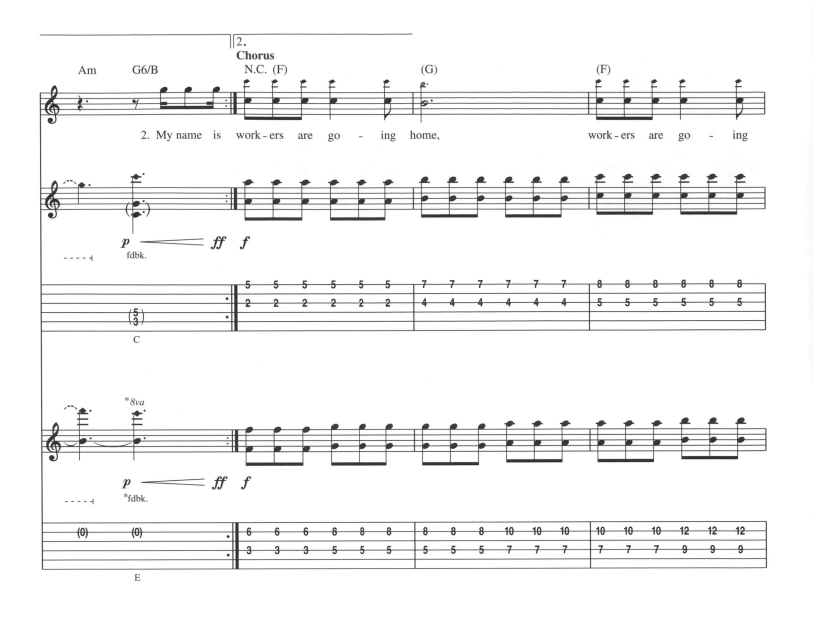

2. My name is work-ers are go-ing home, work-ers are go-ing

home. The work-ers are go-ing home, the work-ers are go-ing

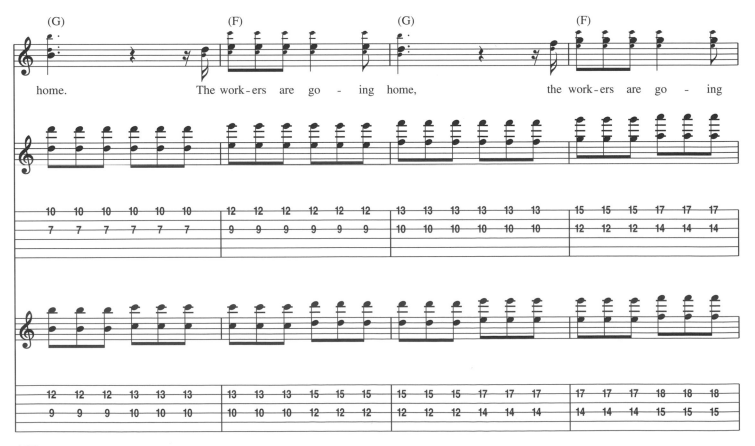

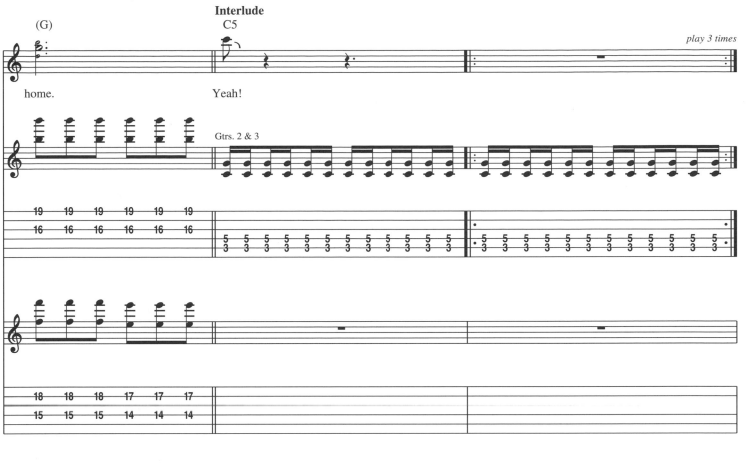

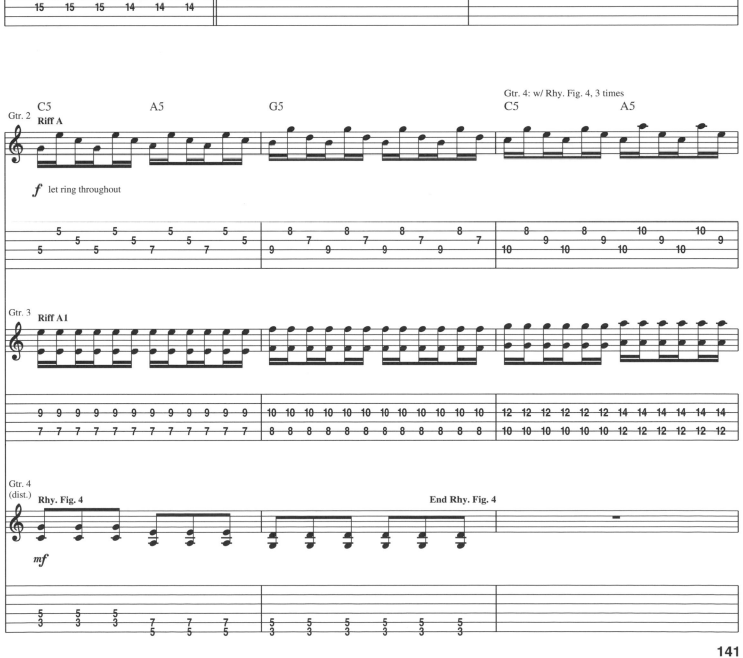

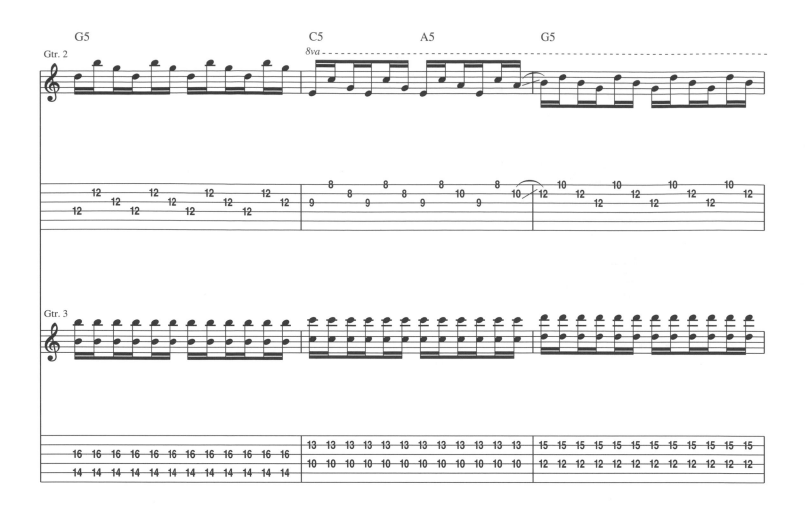

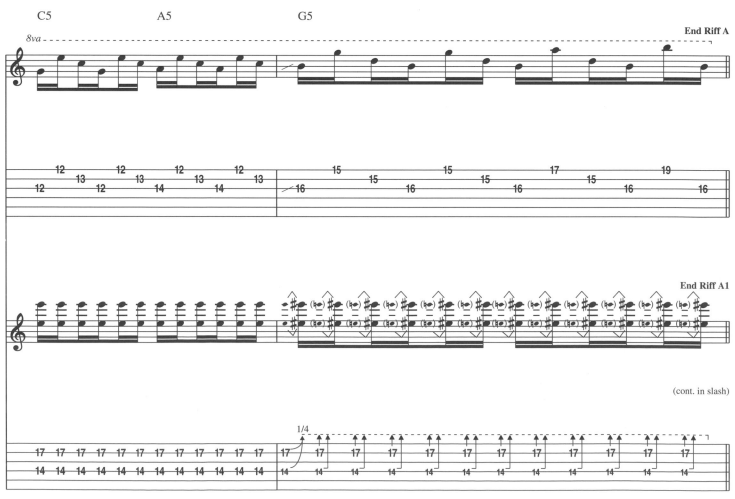

Name

Words and Music by John Rzeznik

Tuning:
①= E ④= E
②= E ⑤= A
③= A ⑥= D

Intro
Moderately Fast Half-Time Feel ♩ = 148

tossed a - long___ the way.___
get to be___ a star?___

And
And

Gtr. 1 w/ Rhy. Fill 1
Gtr. 2: w/ Rhy. Fig. 2, 1st 7 meas.

let - ters that___ you nev - er meant___ to send,___
don't it make___ you sad___ er to know___ that life___

get
is

End Half-Time Feel

Gtr. 2: w/ Rhy. Fill 1, 1st time
Gtrs. 1 & 2: w/ Rhy. Fill 2, 2nd time

lost or thrown___ a - way.___
more than who___ we are?___

And
We

Chorus

now we're grown___ up or - phans___ that nev - er knew___ their names.___
grew up way___ too fast___ and now there's noth - in' to___ be - lieve.___

We

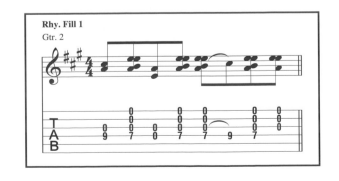

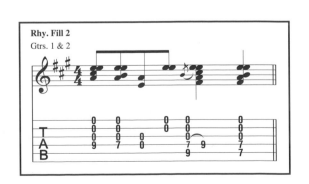

146

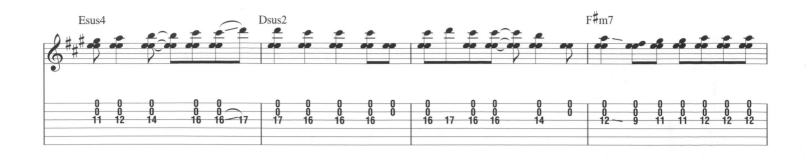

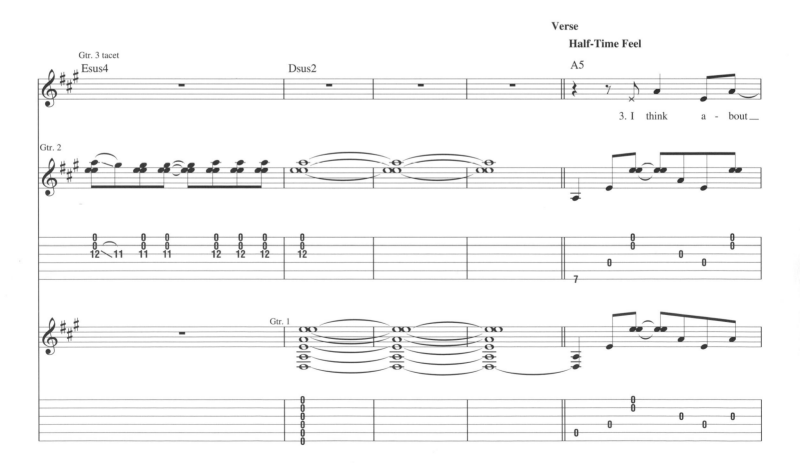

Night Moves

Words and Music by Bob Seger

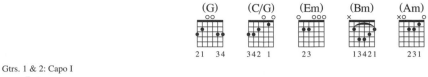

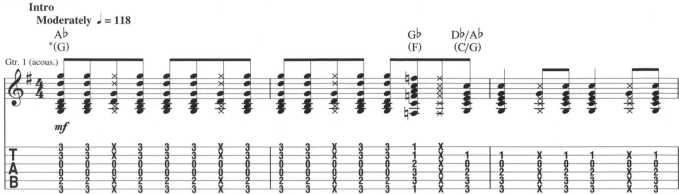

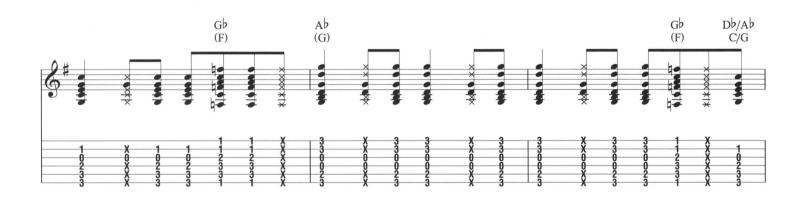

*Symbols in parentheses represent chord names respective to capoed guitar.
Symbols above reflect actual sounding chords. Capoed fret is "0" in tab.

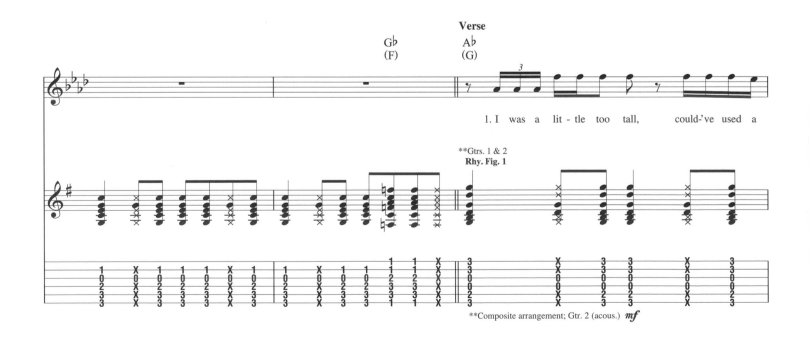

Verse

1. I was a lit-tle too tall, could-'ve used a

**Composite arrangement; Gtr. 2 (acous.) mf

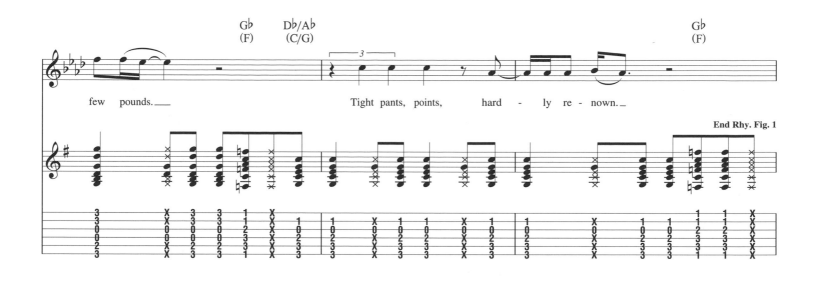

few pounds.___   Tight pants, points, hard - ly re - nown.___

End Rhy. Fig. 1

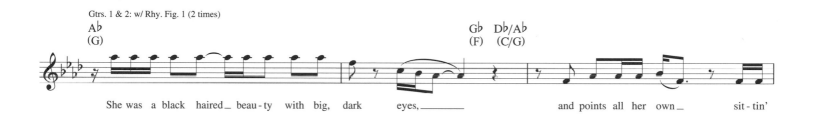

Gtrs. 1 & 2: w/ Rhy. Fig. 1 (2 times)

She was a black haired_ beau - ty with big, dark eyes,___   and points all her own_ sit - tin'

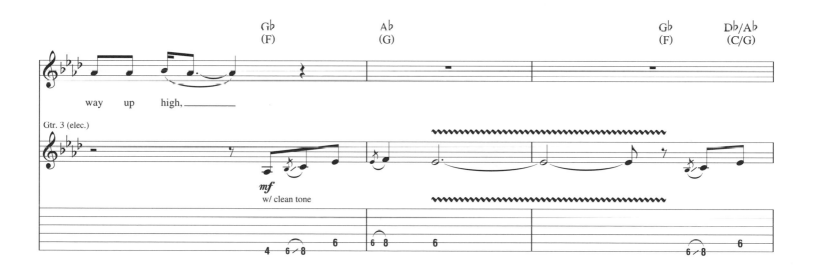

way up high,___

Gtr. 3 (elec.)

mf
w/ clean tone

Verse
Gtrs. 1 & 2: w/ Rhy. Fig. 1 (1 3/4 times)

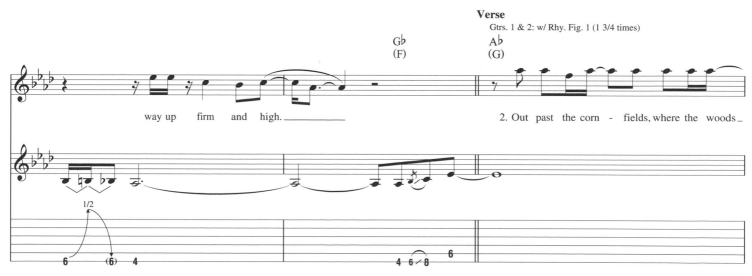

way up firm and high.___   2. Out past the corn - fields, where the woods_

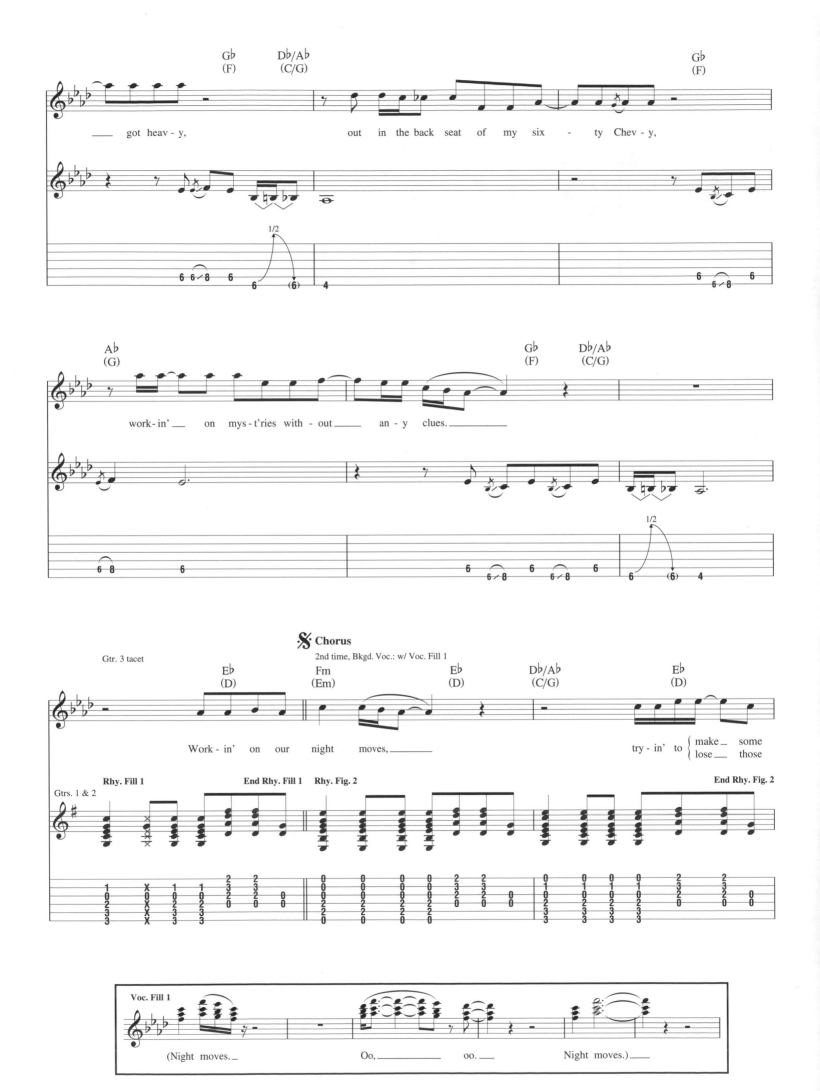

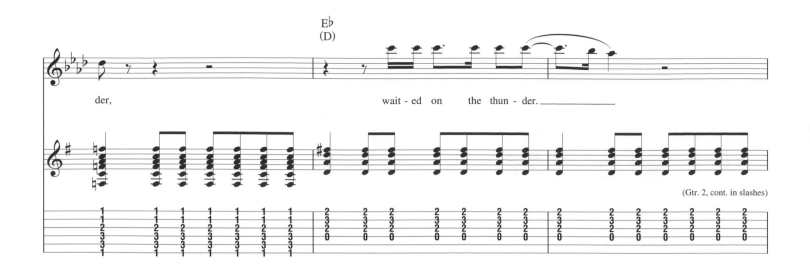

der,   wait-ed on the thun-der. _____

(Gtr. 2, cont. in slashes)

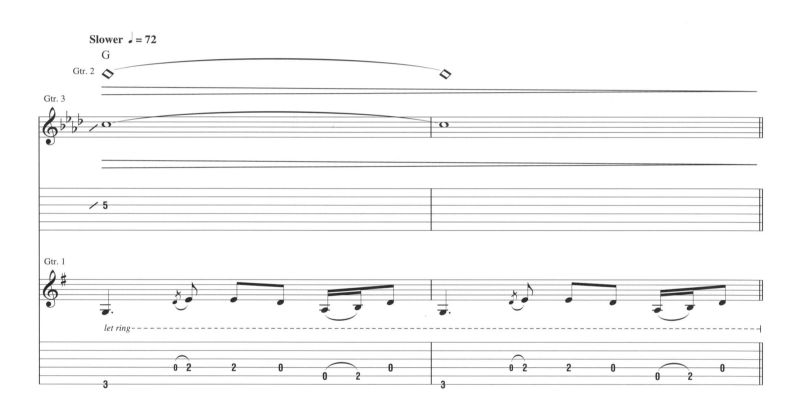

Slower ♩ = 72

Verse
Free time
Gtrs. 2 & 3 tacet

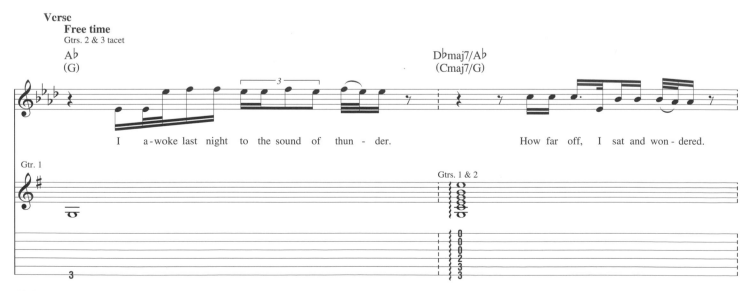

I a-woke last night to the sound of thun-der.   How far off, I sat and won-dered.

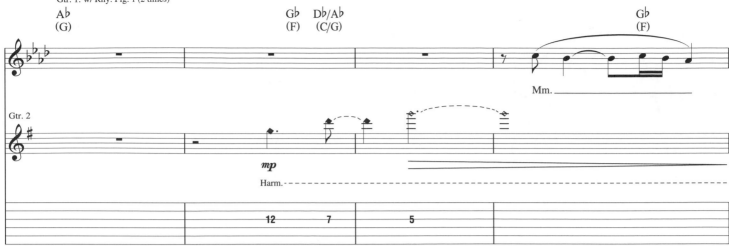

Pitch: G

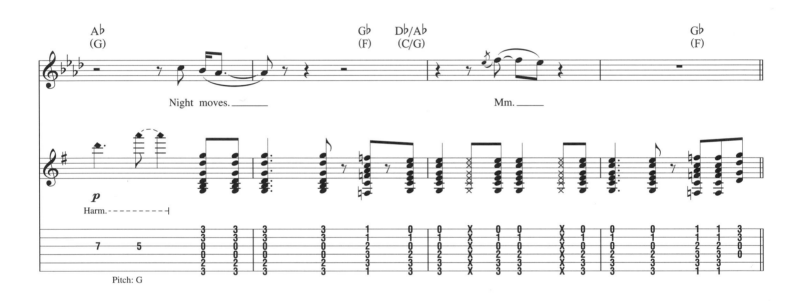

Pitch: G

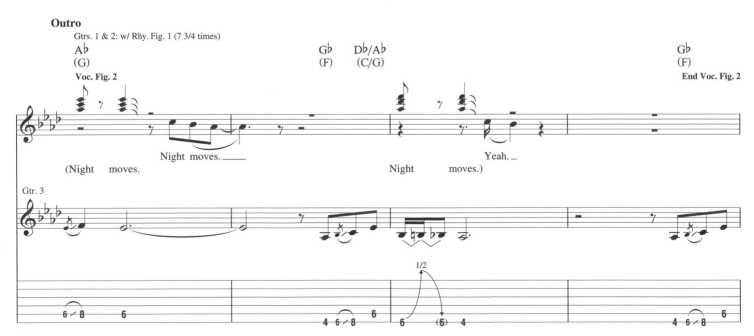

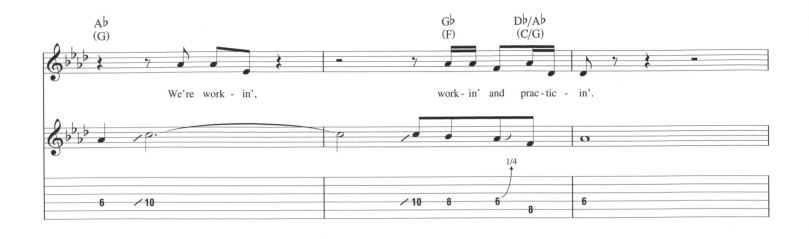

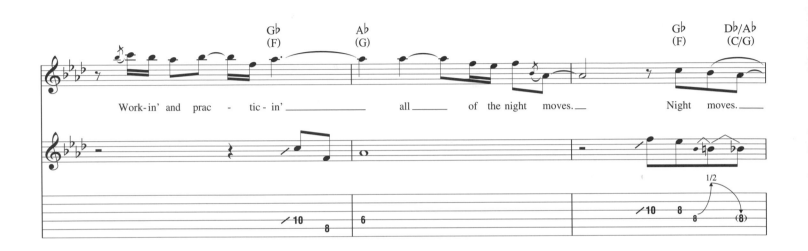

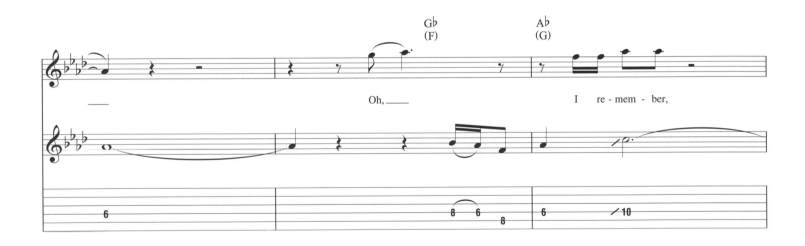

No Rain

Words and Music by Blind Melon

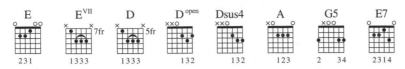

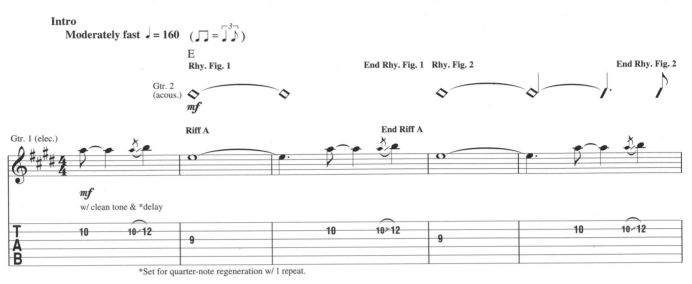

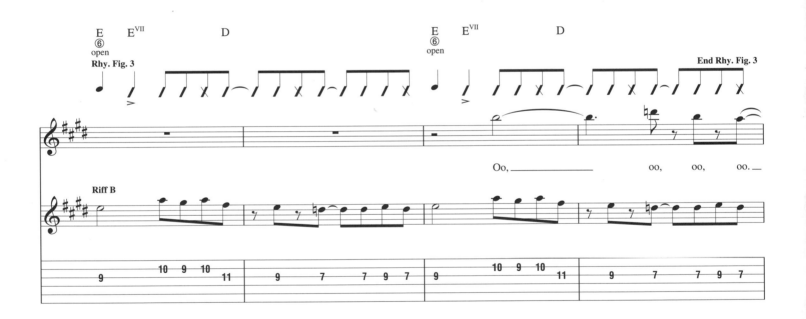

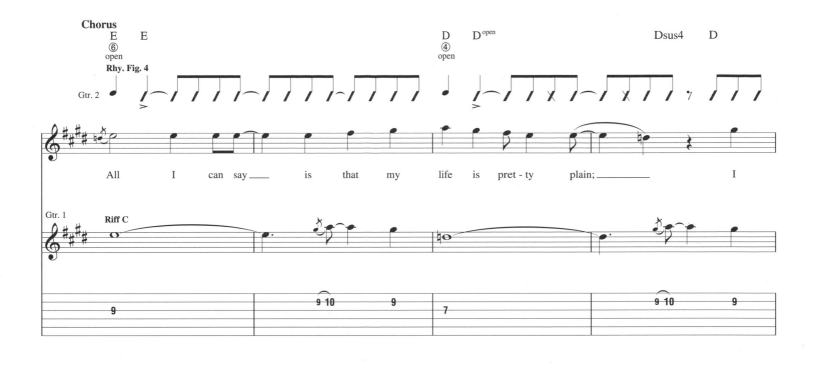

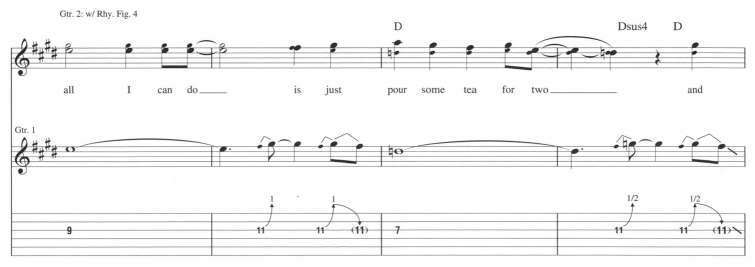

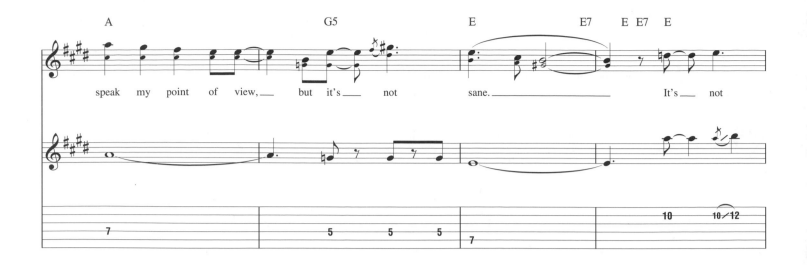

speak my point of view, _____ but it's _____ not sane. _____ It's _____ not

Gtr. 1: w/ Riff A
Gtr. 2: w/ Rhy. Fig. 2

𝄋 **Verse**

Gtr. 1: w/ Riff B (1 3/4 times)
Gtr. 2: w/ Rhy. Fig. 3 (4 times)

E   D

sane. _____   1., 2. I just want some - one to

E   D   E   D

say   to   me, _____   oh,   oh,   oh,   oh, _____   "I'll   al - ways   be _____

E   D

_____ there   when _____ you   wake." _____   Oh,   yeah. _____

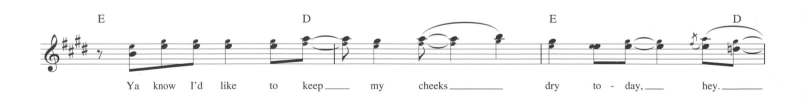

E   D   E   D

Ya   know   I'd   like   to   keep _____ my   cheeks _____   dry   to - day, _____   hey. _____

To Coda ⊕

E   D

_____   So   stay   with   me _____   and   I'll   have   it   made.

Chorus

Gtr. 1: w/ Riff C
Gtr. 2: w/ Rhy. Fig. 4 (1 1/2 times)

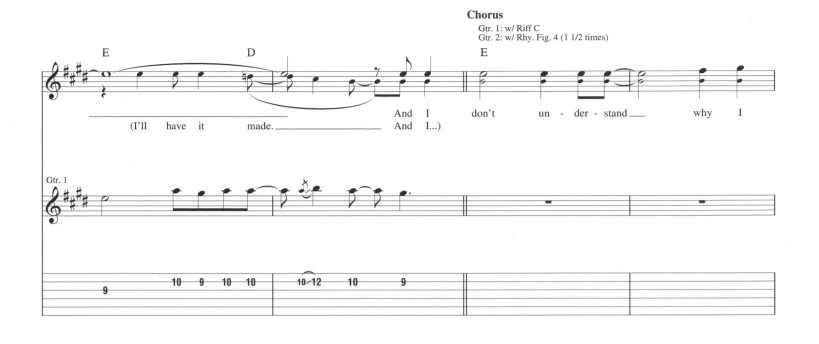

(I'll have it made._____ And I...)
And I don't un - der - stand____ why I

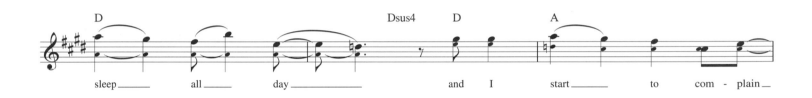

sleep_____ all_____ day_____ and I start_____ to com - plain____

____ that there's____ no_____ rain._____ And

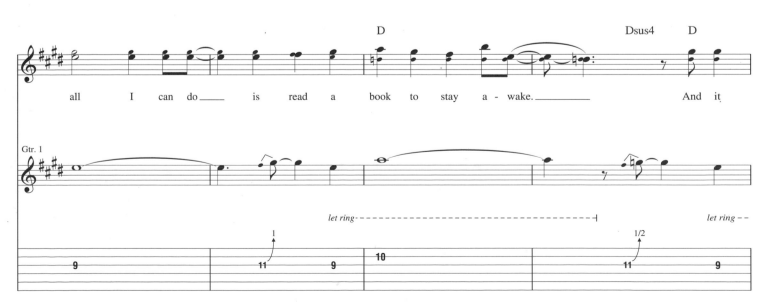

all I can do____ is read a book to stay a - wake._____ And it

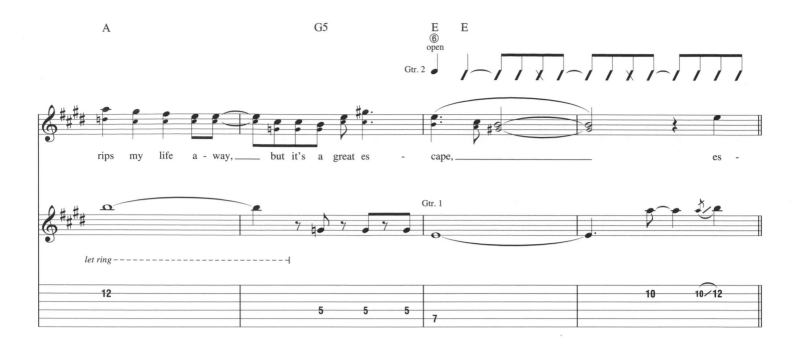

rips my life a - way, _____ but it's a great es - cape, _____ es -

cape, _____ es - cape. _____

Guitar Solo

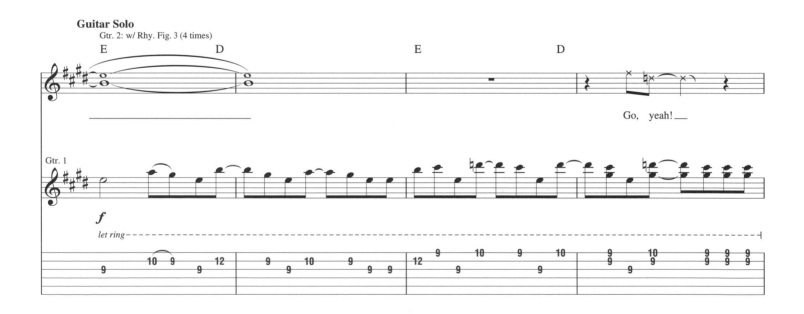

Go, yeah! _____

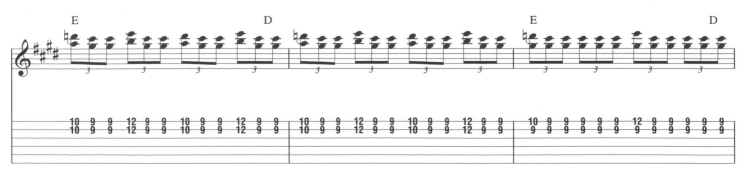

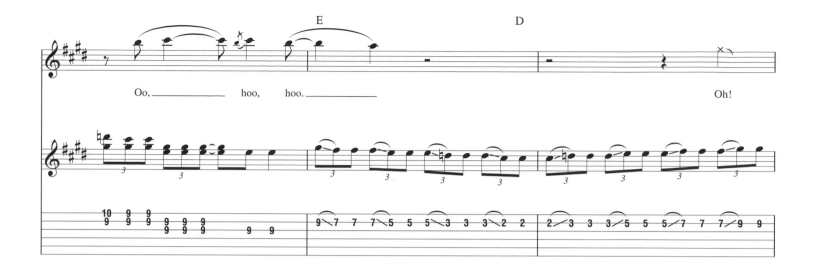

Oo, _____ hoo, hoo. _____ Oh!

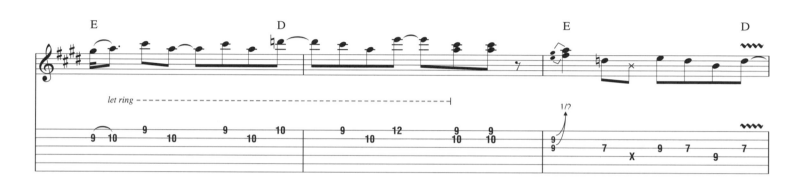

Chorus

All   I   can say ____ is that my   life is pret - ty plain. ____   You   don't

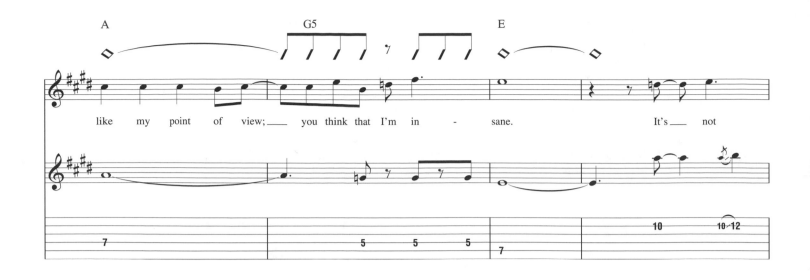

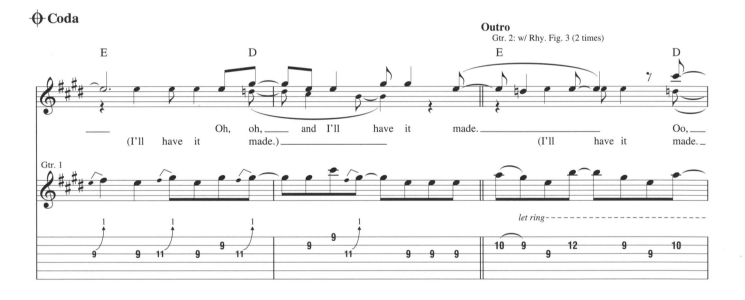

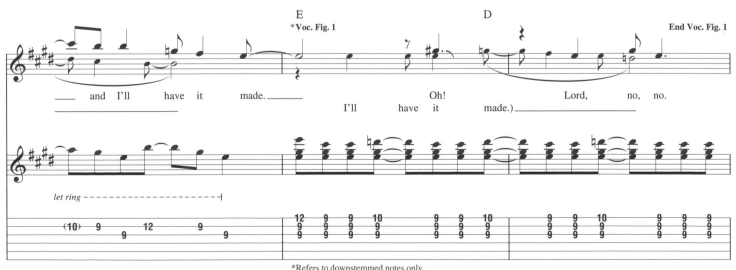

*Refers to downstemmed notes only.

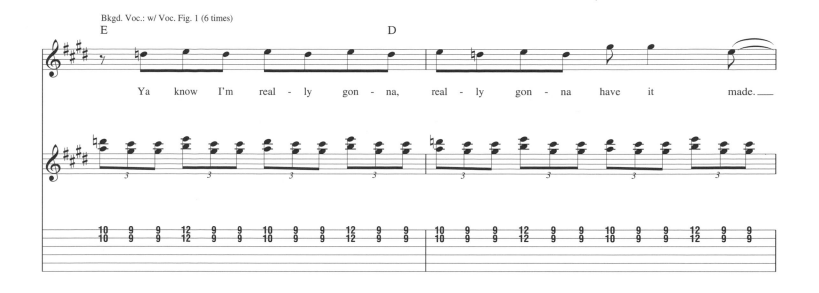

Ya know I'm real - ly gon - na, real - ly gon - na have it made. ____

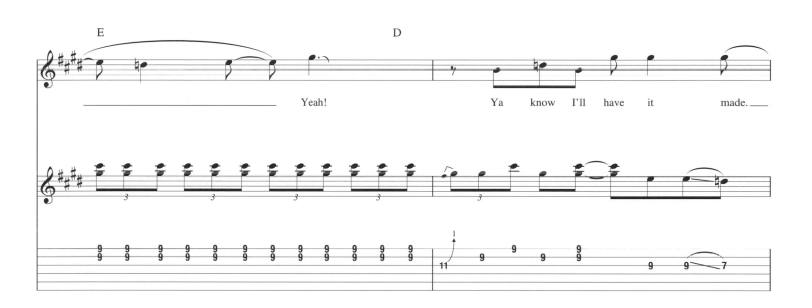

____ Yeah!   Ya know I'll have it made. ____

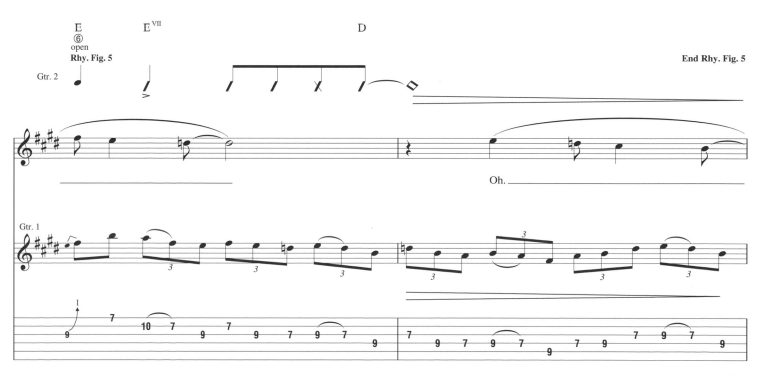

Oh. ____

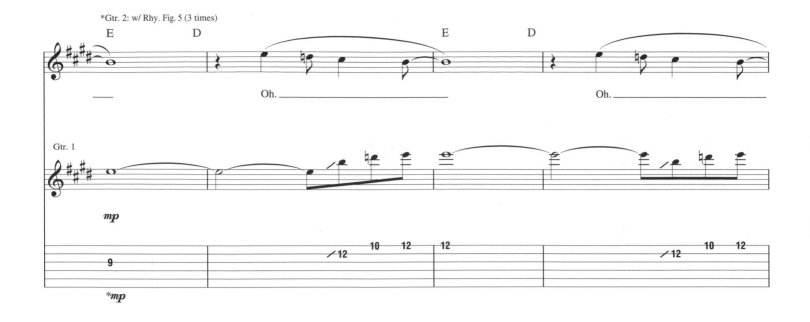

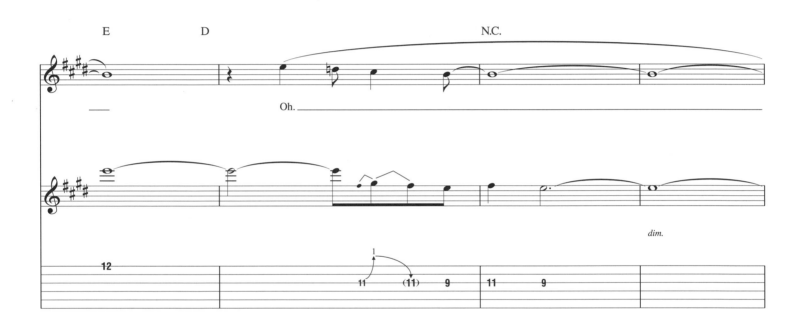

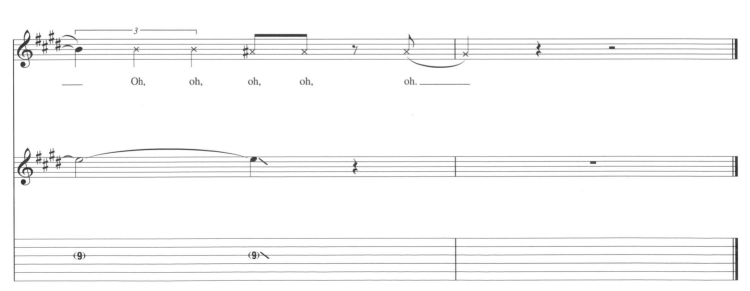

Not Fade Away

Words and Music by Charles Hardin and Norman Petty

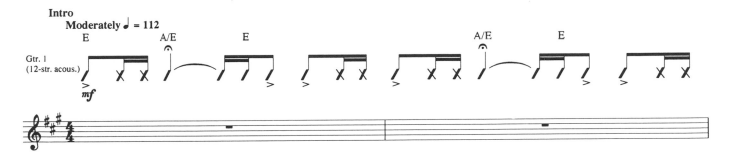

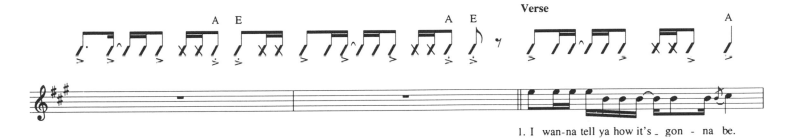

1. I wan-na tell ya how it's _ gon - na be.

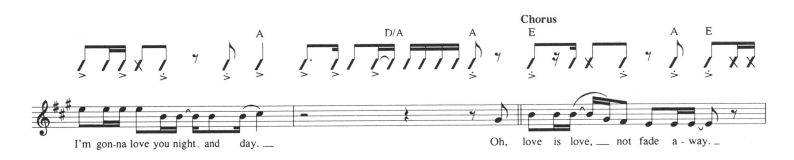

Uh, you're gon-na give your love to me.

I'm gon-na love you night. and day. _   Oh, love is love, _ not fade a - way. _

Uh, well, love is love, _ not fade - a - way. _   2. Uh,

Verse

my love's big-ger than a Cad-il-lac. ___ I ___ try to show it and you drive me back. ___

Uh, your love for me has got ___ to be real, ___

for you to know just how I feel. Uh, love real, ___ not fade a-way. ___

Chorus

Uh, well, love real, ___ not fade a-way. ___   Yeah!

Interlude

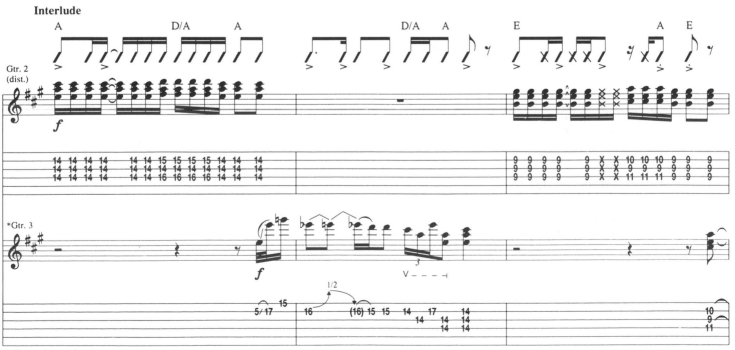

* Harmonica arr. for gtr.

3. I'm gon-na tell ya how it's ___ gon - na be. ___   Uh ___

your gon-na give your love to me.   A love that lasts ___ more than one day. ___

Chorus

Uh well, love is love, ___ not fade a - way. ___   Well,

Outro

love is love, ___ not fade a - way. ___   Well, love is love, ___ not fade a - way. ___

Begin Fade

L - love, love, 'll not fade a - way. ___   Not
(Love, love, ___ not fade a - way.) ___   (Not

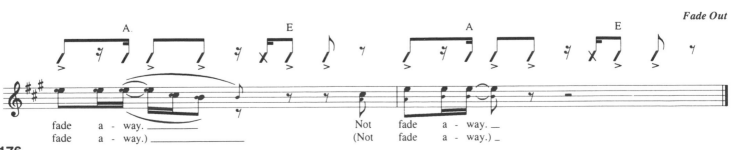

Fade Out

fade a - way. ___
(fade a - way.) ___   Not fade a - way. ___
                    (Not fade a - way.) ___

Oh Well Part 1

Words and Music by Peter Alan Green

*Chord symbols reflect overall harmony.

**Play 2nd time only (next 3 bars).

Verse

Gtrs. 1 & 2 tacet

Gtr. 3 tacet

N.C.(Em)

1. I can't help a-bout the shape I'm in. __ I can't sing, I ain't pret-ty and my legs are thin. __

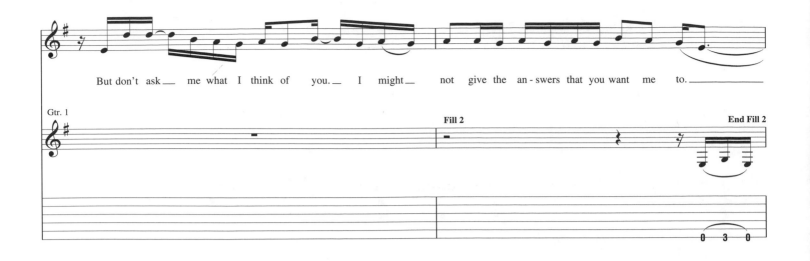

But don't ask___ me what I think of you.___ I might___ not give the an-swers that you want me to._____

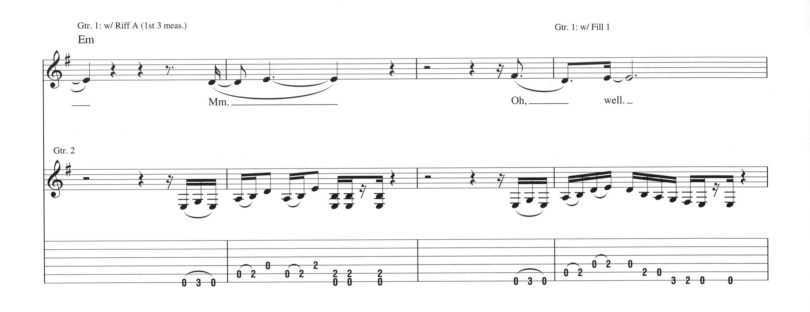

Mm._____ Oh,_____ well.___

Verse

2. Now, when I _____ talked to God I knew He'd un-der - stand.__ He said,

stick by me __ and I'll be your__ guid-ing hand.__ But don't ask __ me what I think of you.__ I might

not give the an-swer that you want me to. _____ Mm.__

Pink Houses

Words and Music by John Mellencamp

G5   F6sus2   Cadd9

(Oh, _____ oh, _____ oh, _____ yeah.) __

let ring

D.S. al Coda 2

G5

Gtr. 1

(cont. in notation)

3. Well, there's peo -

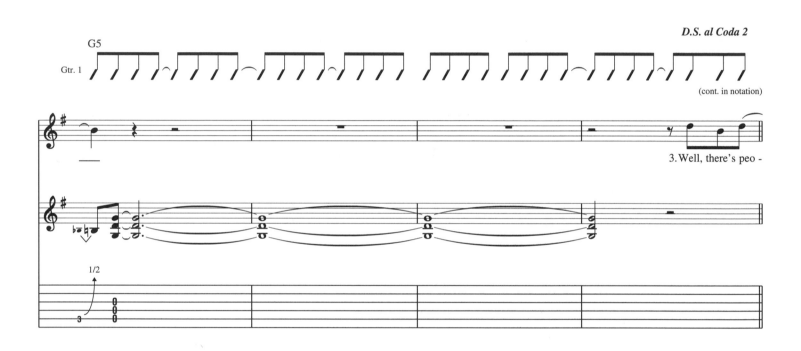

✛ **Coda 2**

F6/9   Cadd9 type2   G

Gtr. 1

- ple, man, __ ba - by, pays for the thrills, __ the bills, the pills that kill. __
(Ooh.) _____

Gtr. 2

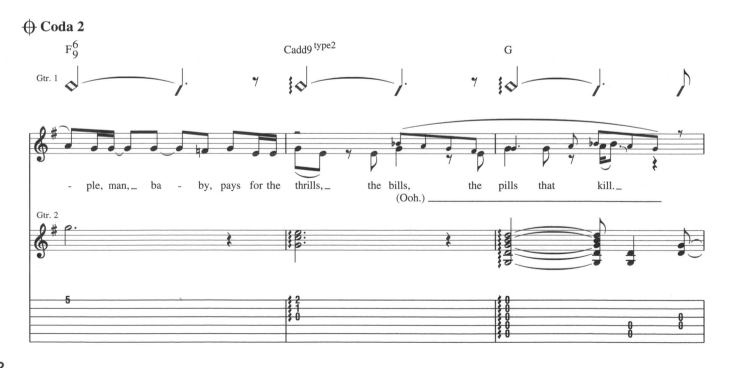

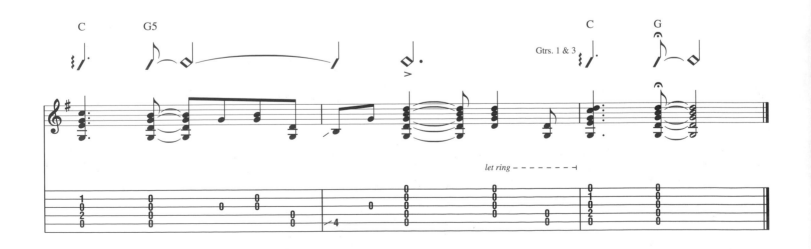

Run Around

Words and Music by John Popper

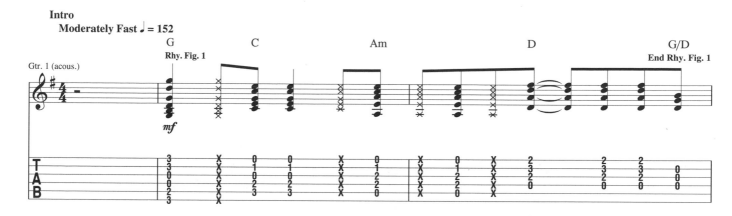

1. Oh, _____ once up - on _____ a mid -
2. *See additional lyrics*

- night dear - ie I woke with some - thing in my head. _____ I

could - n't es - cape the _____ mem - o - ry _____ of a phone call and of what you

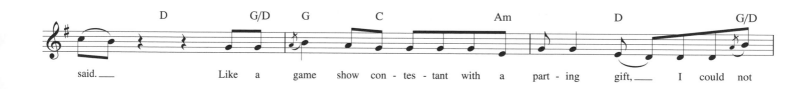

said. _____ Like a game show con - tes - tant with a part - ing gift, _____ I could not

be - lieve _____ my _____ eyes _____ when I saw through the voice _____ of a trust -

Additional Lyrics

2. And shake me and my confidence
   About a great many things,
   But I've been there, I can see it cower
   Like a nervous magician waiting in the wings
   Of a bad play where the heroes are right
   And nobody thinks or expects too much.
   And Hollywood's calling for the movie rights,
   Singing, "Hey babe, let's keep in touch.
   Hey baby, let's keep in touch."
   But I want more than a touch, I want you to reach me
   And show me all the things no one else can see.
   So what you feel becomes mine as well.
   And soon, if we're lucky, we'd be unable to tell
   What's yours and mine, the fishing's fine,
   And it doesn't have to rhyme, so don't you feed me a line.

Seven Bridges Road

Words and Music by Stephen T. Young

Drop D tuning:
(low to high): D-A-D-G-B-E

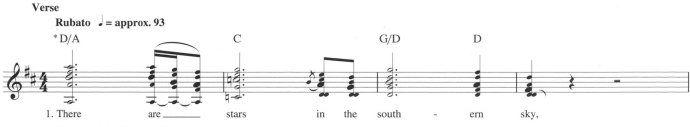

Verse
Rubato ♩ = approx. 93

1. There are _____ stars in the south - ern sky,

*Chord symbols reflect impled harmony

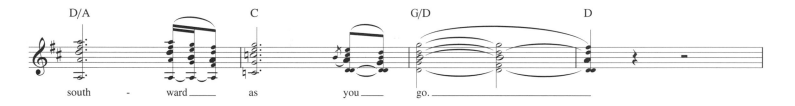

south - ward _____ as you _____ go. _____

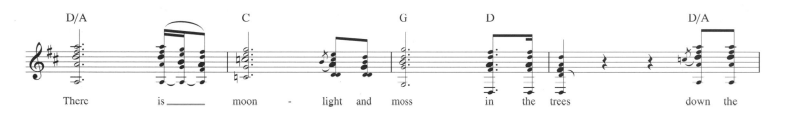

There is _____ moon - light and moss in the trees down the

Interlude
Faster ♩ = 111

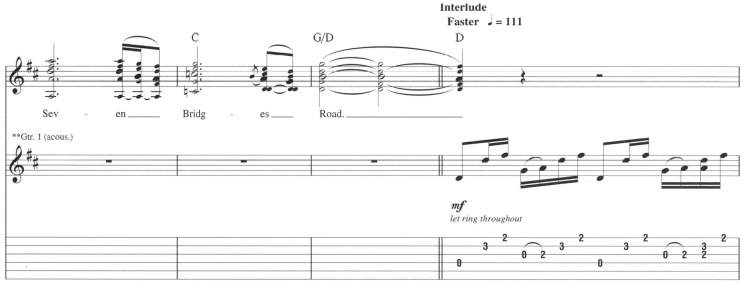

Sev - en _____ Bridg - es _____ Road. _____

Gtr. 1 (acous.)

mf
let ring throughout

**Two gtrs. (6 & 12-str. acous.) arr. for one.

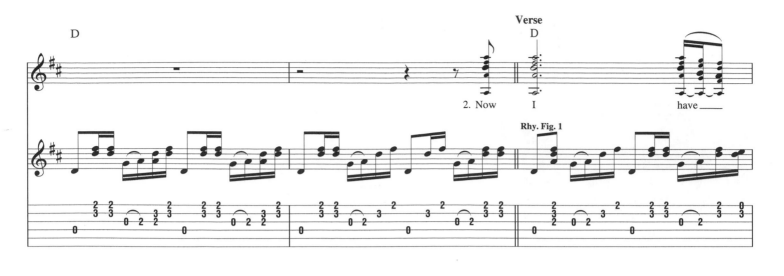

2. Now   I   have ____

loved ____   you ____ like a ba - by,

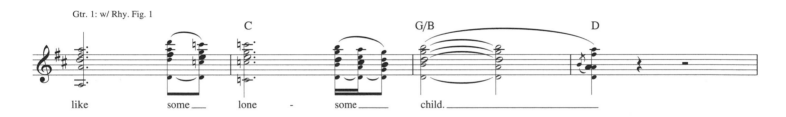

like   some ____ lone - some ____ child. ____

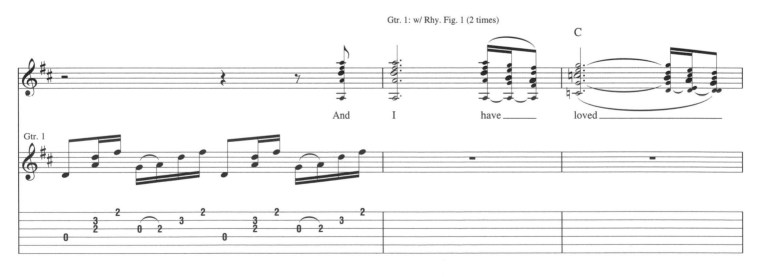

And   I   have ____ loved ____

you ____   in a tame ____ way,   and I   have ____

200

from these _____ warm stars _____ down the

Sev - en _____ Bridg - es _____ Road.

Verse
Rubato ♩ = approx. 90
Gtr. 1 tacet

3. There are _____ stars in the south - ern sky, and if

ev - er _____ you ___ de - cide you ___ should go, _____

there is a taste of ___ time sweet and hon - ey down the

Sev - en _____ Bridg - es _____ Road.

Slide

Words and Music by John Rzeznik

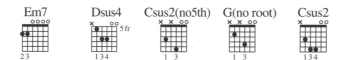

* Tuning:

① = D#   ④ = D#
② = D#   ⑤ = A#
③ = G#   ⑥ = D#

Intro
Moderate Rock ♩ = 114

* All music is notated one half step lower than actual sounding pitch for ease of reading.

Verse

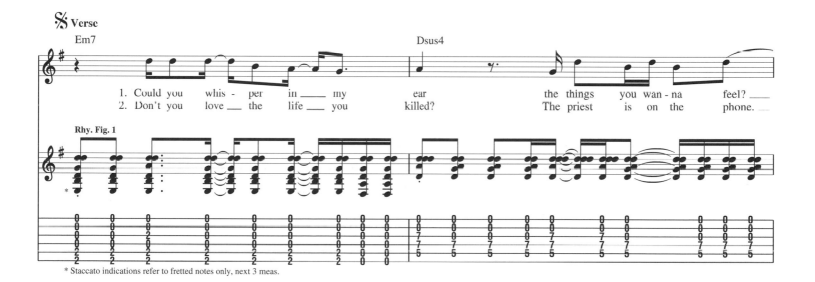

1. Could you whis - per in ___ my ear the things you wan - na feel? ___
2. Don't you love ___ the life ___ you killed? The priest is on the phone.

* Staccato indications refer to fretted notes only, next 3 meas.

___ I'll give you an - y - thing ___ to feel it com - in'.
___ Your fa - ther hit the wall, ___ your ma dis - owned ___ you. ___

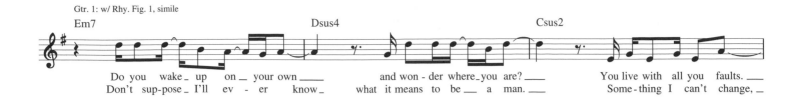

Gtr. 1: w/ Rhy. Fig. 1, simile

Em7   Dsus4   Csus2

Do you wake up on your own   and won-der where you are?   You live with all you faults.
Don't sup-pose I'll ev-er know   what it means to be a man.   Some-thing I can't change,

Pre-Chorus

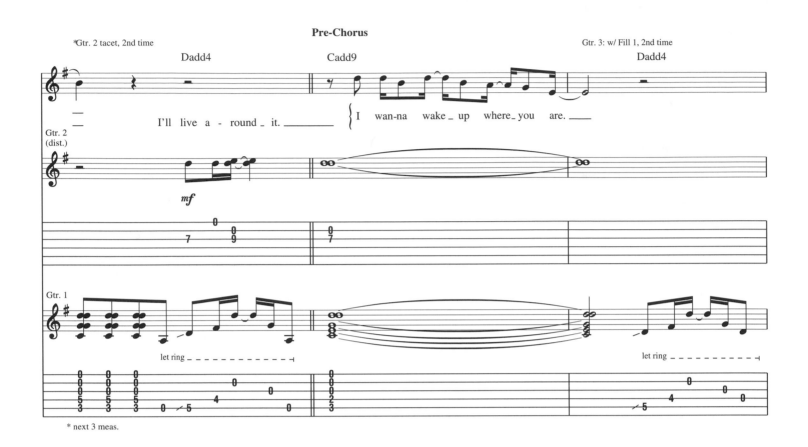

*Gtr. 2 tacet, 2nd time

Dadd4   Cadd9   Gtr. 3: w/ Fill 1, 2nd time   Dadd4

I'll live a-round it.   { I wan-na wake up where you are.

Gtr. 2 (dist.)

mf

Gtr. 1

let ring

* next 3 meas.

To Coda 1

Gtr. 2 tacet

Cadd9

I won't say an-y-thing at all.   So why don't you

Gtr. 1

let ring

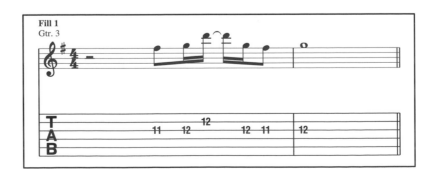

Fill 1
Gtr. 3

is what you are, __ and what you are is beau - ti - ful. __ Oh, May, do you wan-na get __ mar -

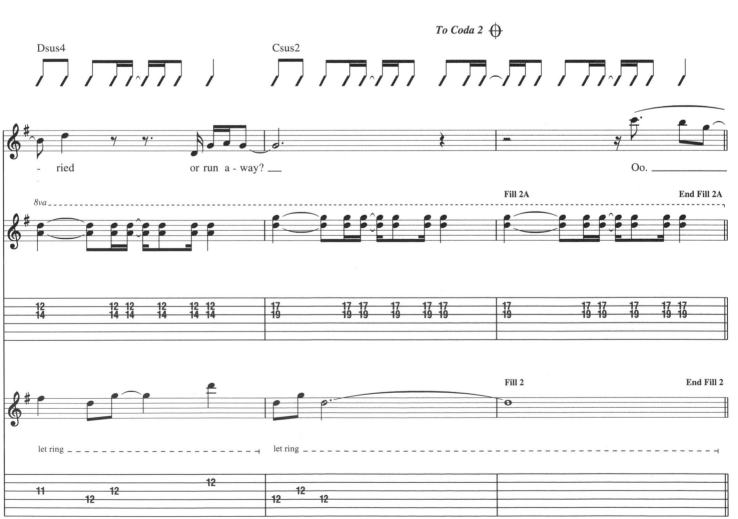

- ried or run a - way? __ Oo. __

Starman

Words and Music by David Bowie

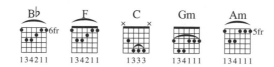

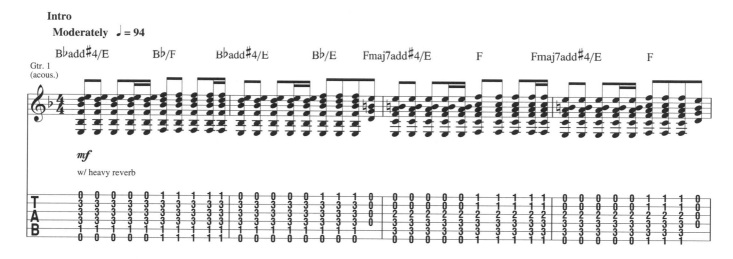

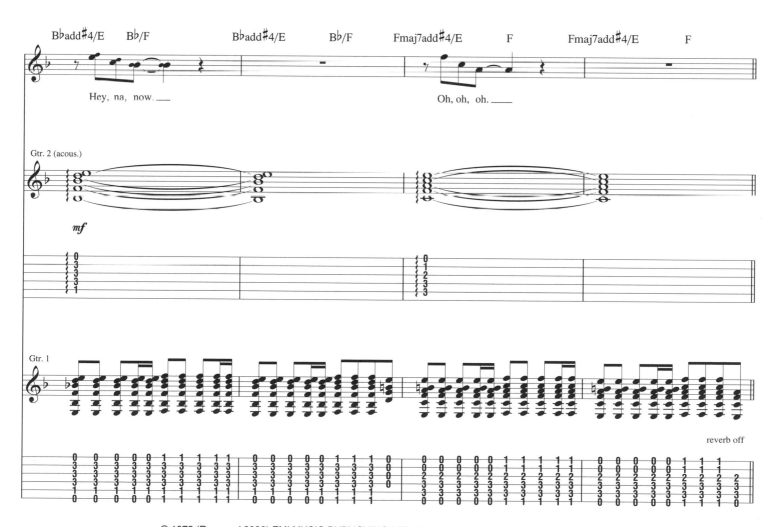

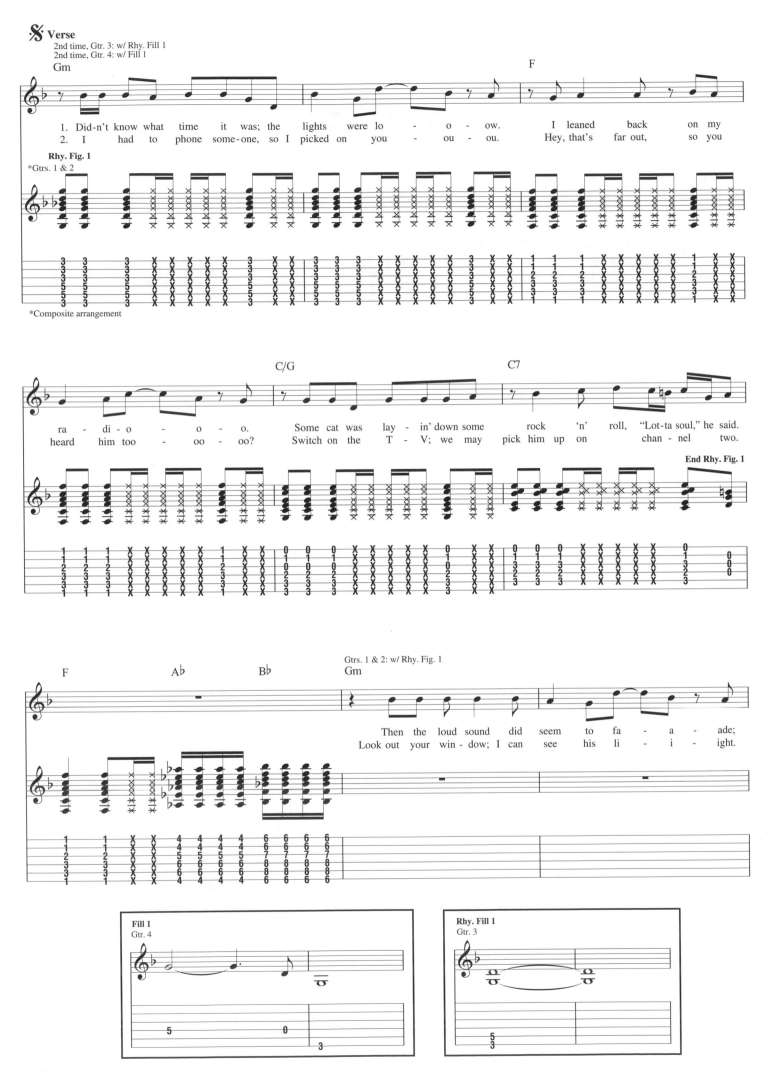

came back like a slow voice on a wave of pha — a — ase. That were-n't no D. J., that was
If he can spar - kle, he may land to - ni - i - ight. Don't tell your pop-pa or he'll

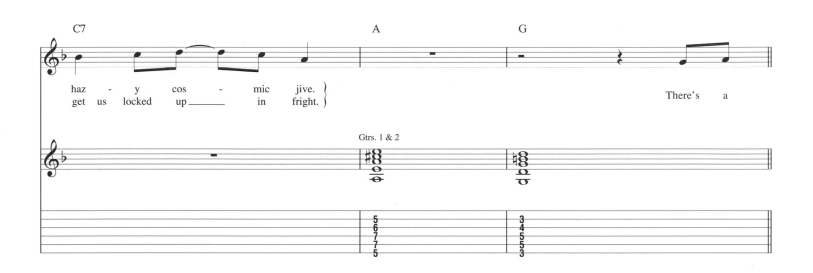

haz - y cos - mic jive.
get us locked up in fright.
There's a

Chorus

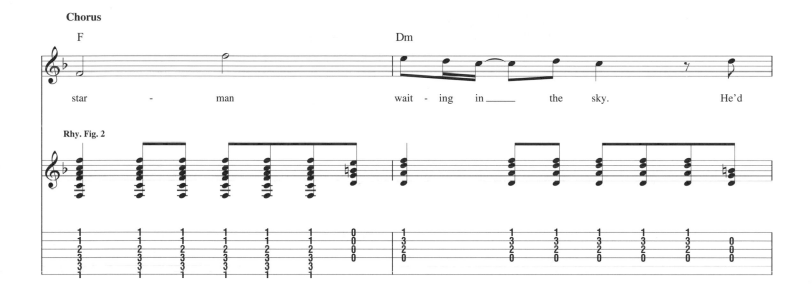

star - man wait - ing in the sky. He'd

Rhy. Fig. 2

like to come and meet us but he thinks he'd blow our minds. There's a

End Rhy. Fig. 2

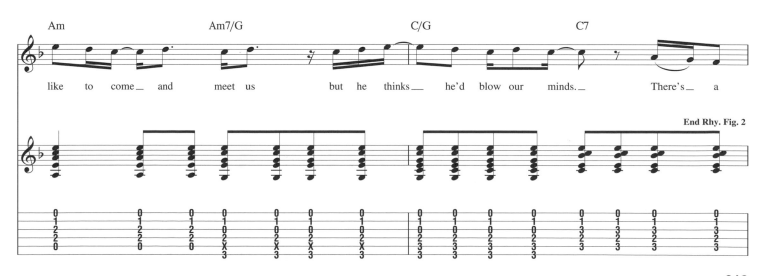

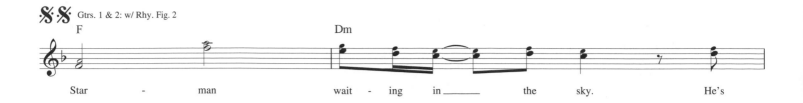

Gtrs. 1 & 2: w/ Rhy. Fig. 2

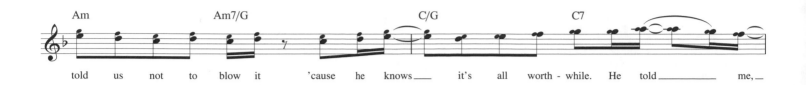

Star - man wait - ing in ___ the sky. He's

told us not to blow it 'cause he knows ___ it's all worth - while. He told ___ me, ___

To Coda 1 ⊕

___ "Let the chil - dren lose it. Let the chil - dren use it. Let all the chil - dren boo - gie."

Gtrs. 1 & 2

(cont. in slashes)

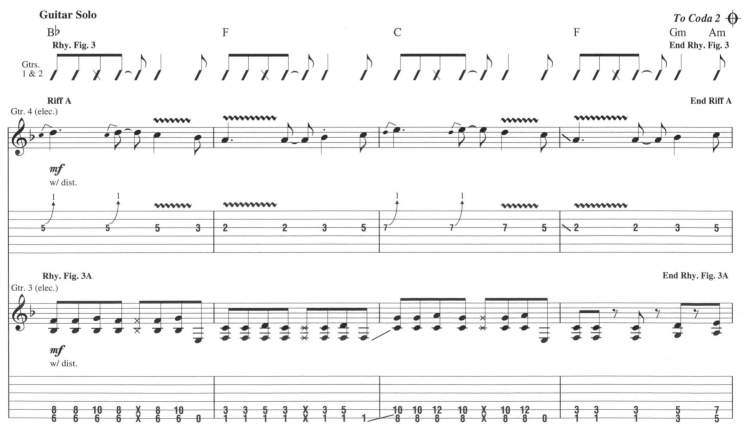

Guitar Solo

To Coda 2 ⊕

214

Gtrs. 1 & 2: w/ Rhy. Fig. 3 (1st 3 meas.)
Gtr. 3: w/ Rhy. Fig. 3A (1st 3 meas.)

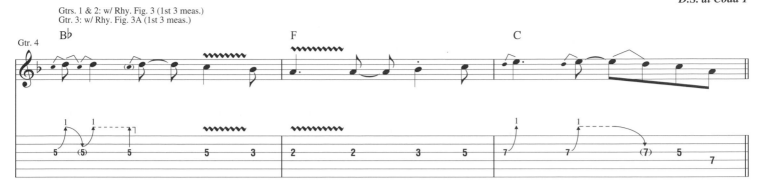

Coda 1

Gtrs. 1 & 2: w/ Rhy. Fig. 2

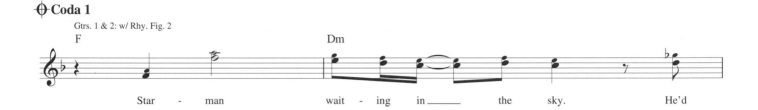

Star - man wait - ing in _____ the sky. He'd

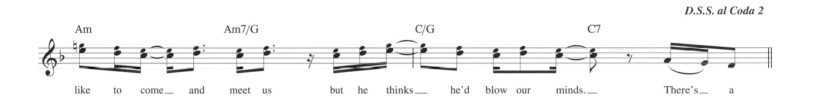

like to come_ and meet us but he thinks_ he'd blow our minds._ There's_ a

Coda 2

Outro

Gtrs. 1 & 2: w/ Rhy. Fig. 3
Gtr. 3: w/ Rhy. Fig. 3A
Gtr. 4: w/ Riff A

La, la,_ la, la, la, la,_ la, la, la, la,_ la, la, la, la,_ la, la.

Voc.: w/ Voc. Fig. 1 (till fade)
Gtrs. 1 & 2: w/ Rhy. Fig. 3 (till fade)
Gtr. 3: w/ Rhy. Fig. 3A (till fade)

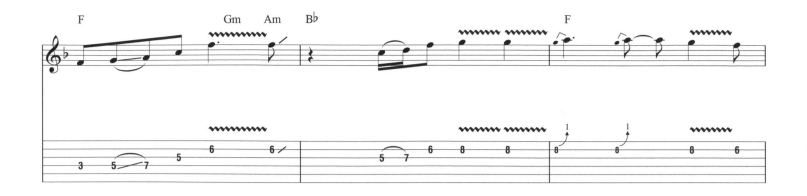

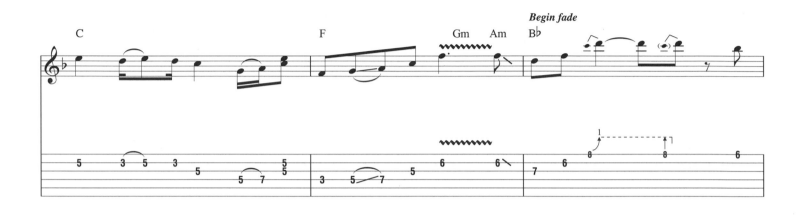

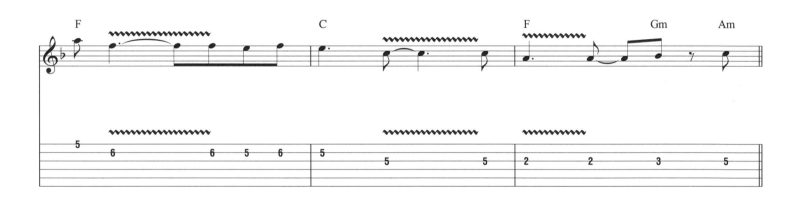

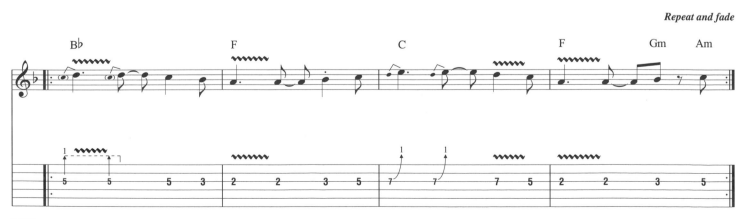

Suite Madame Blue

Words and Music by Dennis DeYoung

Interlude

Faster ♩ = 79

Gtrs 1 & 2 tacet

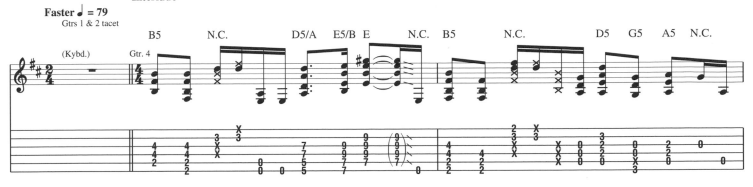

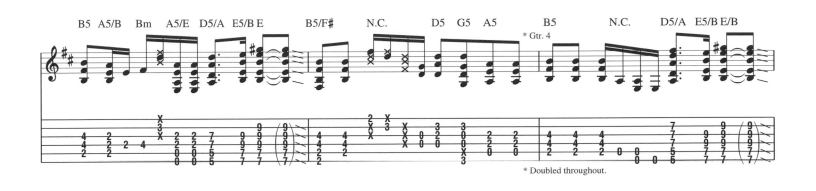

* Doubled throughout.

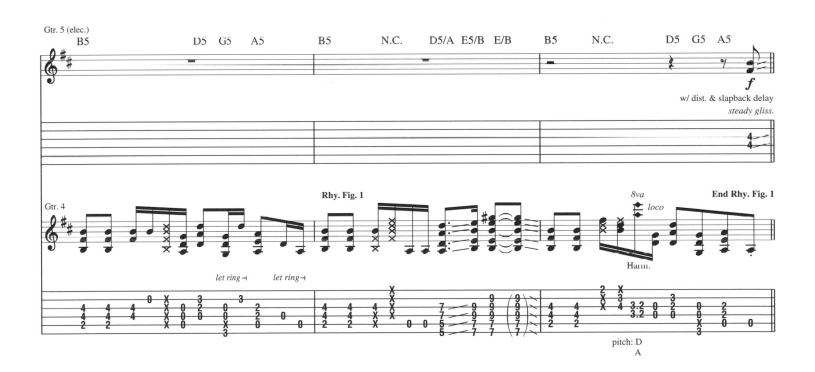

* Gtr. 4

pitch: D
A

Guitar Solo

Gtr. 4: w/ Rhy. Fig. 1 (4 times)

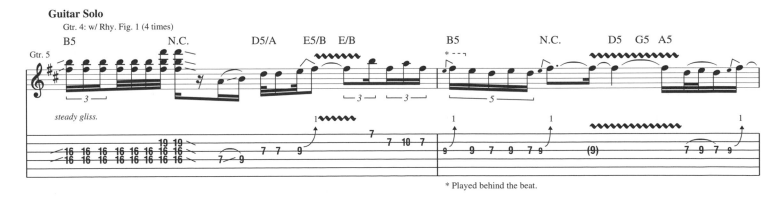

* Played behind the beat.

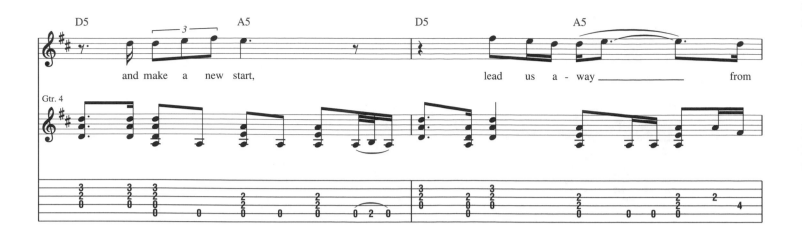

and make a new start, lead us a-way _____ from

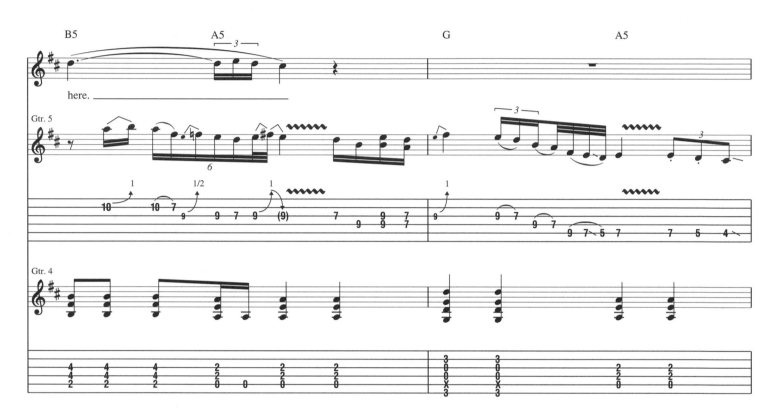

here. _____

Gtrs. 4 & 5 * Bm

* Chord symbols reflect overall harmony.

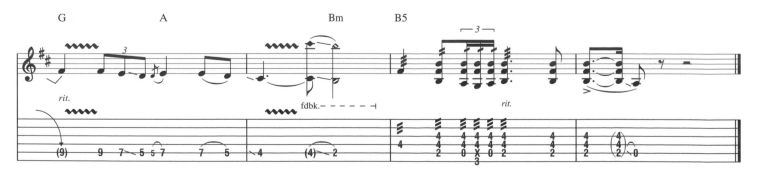

Suite: Judy Blue Eyes

Words and Music by Stephen Stills

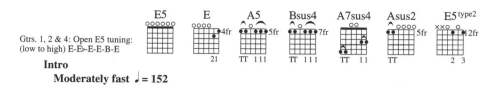

Gtrs. 1, 2 & 4: Open E5 tuning:
(low to high) E-E♭-E-E-B-E

Intro

Moderately fast ♩ = 152

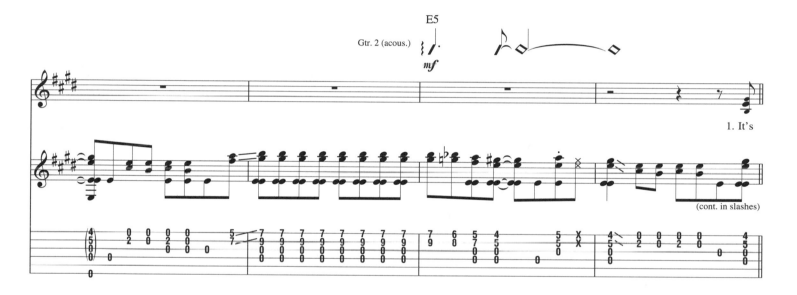

1. It's

(cont. in slashes)

Verse

1st time, Gtr. 2 tacet
2nd time, Gtrs. 1, 2 & 3: w/ Rhy. Fills 2 & 2A

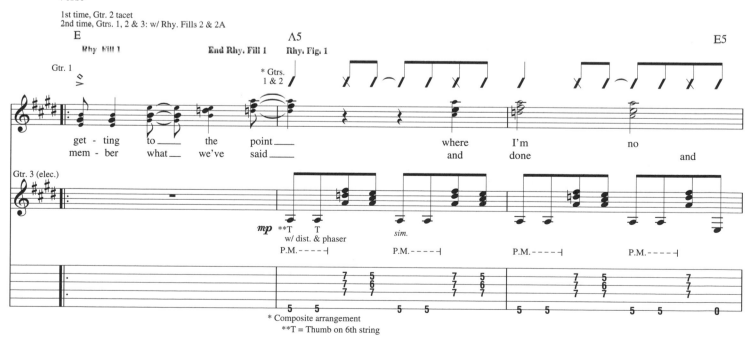

get - ting   to ___   the   point ___   where   I'm   no
mem - ber   what ___   we've   said ___   and   done   and

Gtr. 3 (elec.)

w/ dist. & phaser

* Composite arrangement
**T = Thumb on 6th string

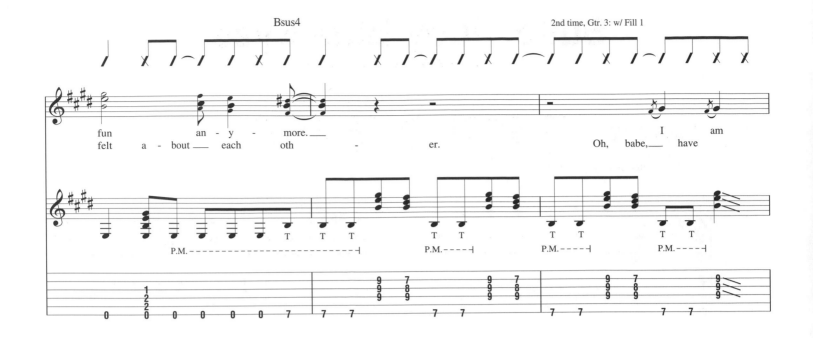

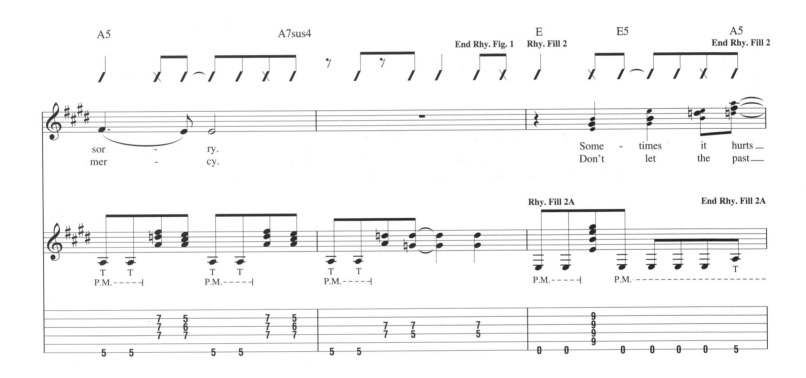

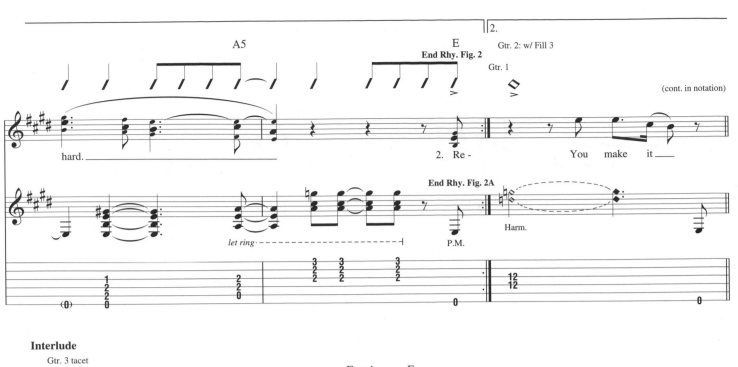

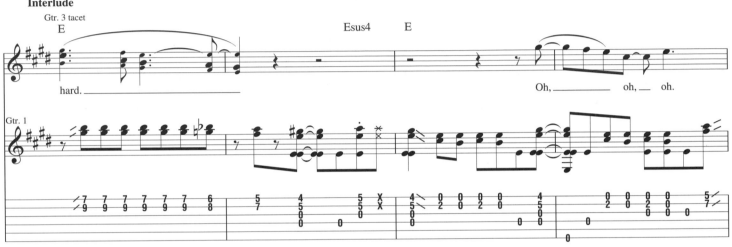

Interlude

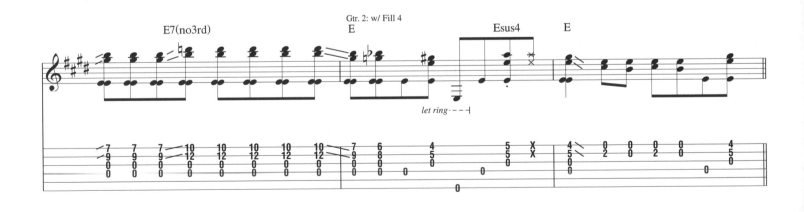

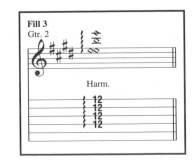

Bridge

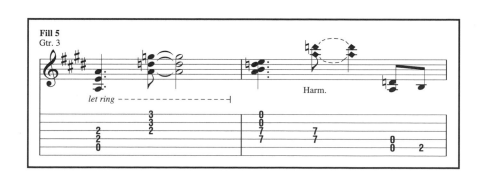

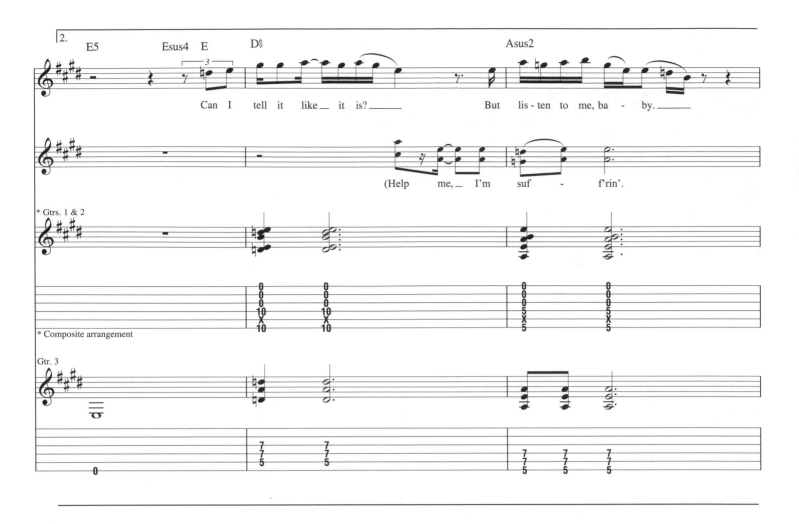

Verse

5. Chest-nut brown_ ca-nar y,_ ru-by throat-ed spar-
6. Voic-es of _ the an - gels, _ ring a - round the moon-

Gtrs. 1 & 2

let ring

Composite arrangement

2nd time, Gtrs. 1 & 2: w/ Rhy. Fill 3

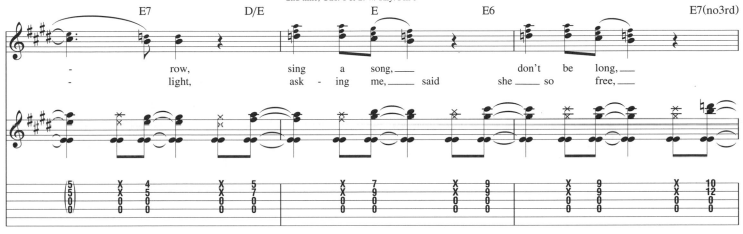

- row, sing a song,_ don't be long,_
- light, ask-ing me,_ said she _ so free,_

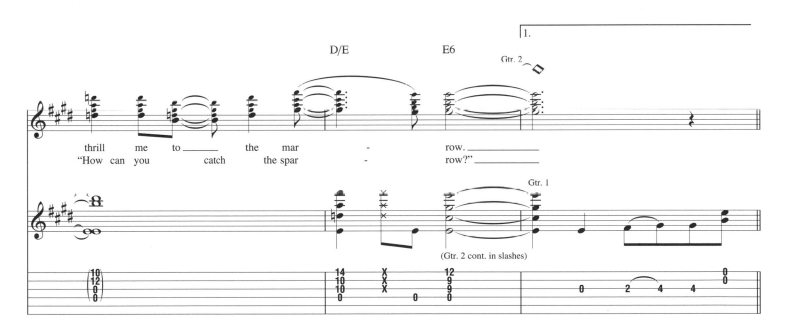

thrill me to _ the mar - row. _
"How can you catch the spar - gels-row?" _

Gtr. 2

Gtr. 1

(Gtr. 2 cont. in slashes)

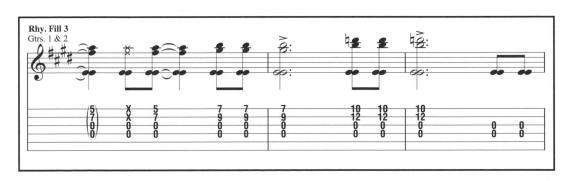

Rhy. Fill 3
Gtrs. 1 & 2

Guitar Solo

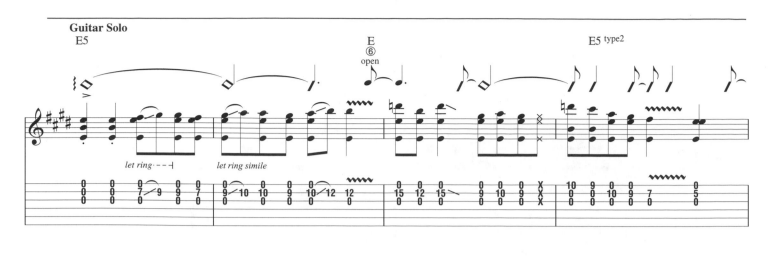

(cont. in notation)

* Hit body of gtr.

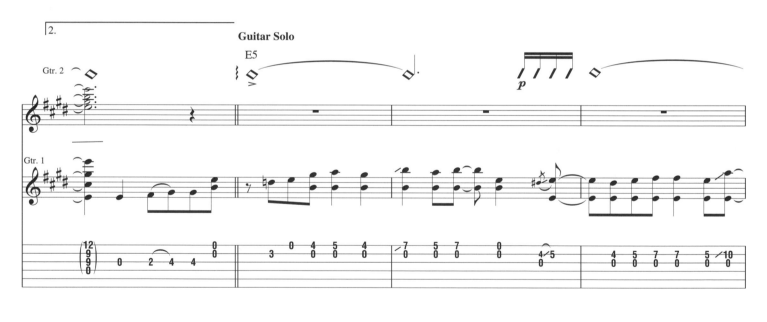

Guitar Solo

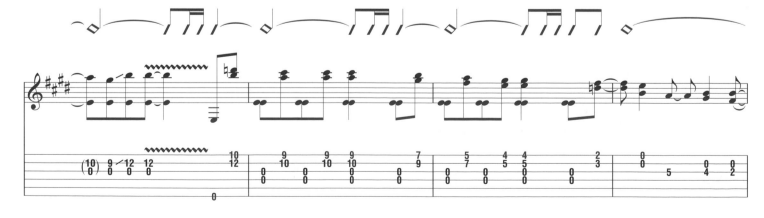

Verse

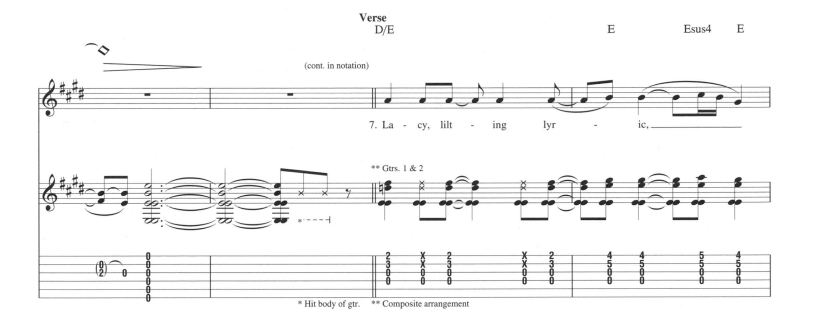

(cont. in notation)

7. La - cy, lilt - ing lyr - ic, _____

** Gtrs. 1 & 2

* Hit body of gtr.   ** Composite arrangement

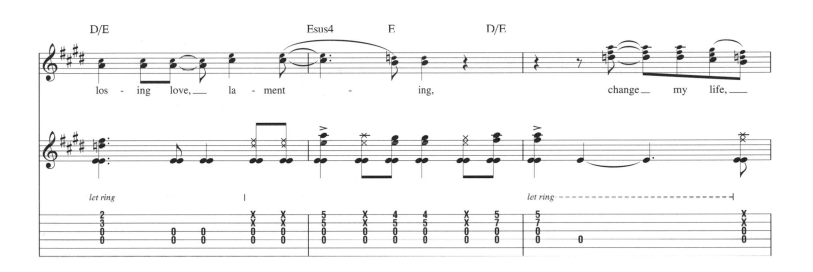

los - ing love, __ la - ment - ing, __ change __ my life, __

let ring

let ring - - - - - - - - - - - - - - - - -

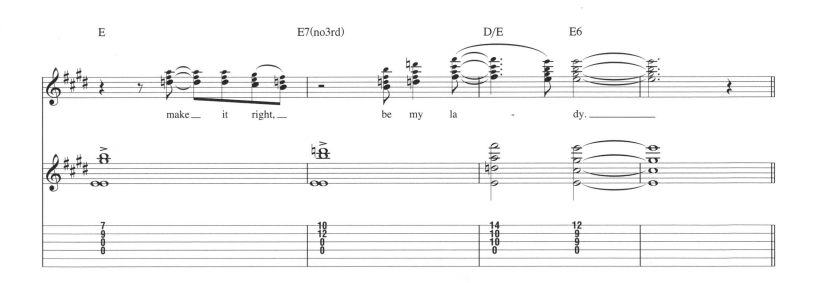

make __ it right, __ be my la - dy. __

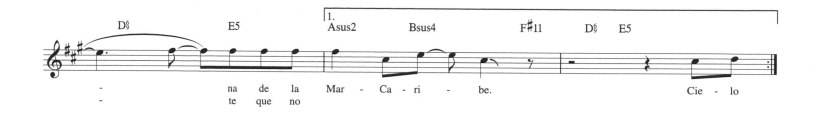

na de la Mar - Ca - ri - be.   Cie - lo

te que no

pue - do va - ya. Oh,___ va! Oh, va! Do, do, do, do, do, do, do, do, do, do, do.

Do, do, do, do, do, do, do, do, do.   do, do, do.

Additional Lyrics

Bridge:

3. I've got an answer,
   I'm going to fly away.
   What have I got to lose?

4. Will you come see me
   Thursdays and Saturdays? Hey, (hey,) hey.
   What have you got to lose?

Outro translation:
How happy it makes me to think of Cuba,
The smiles of the Caribbean Sea.
Sunny sky has no blood,
And how sad that I'm not able to go.
Oh, go! Oh, go!

Sweet Jane

Words and Music by Lou Reed

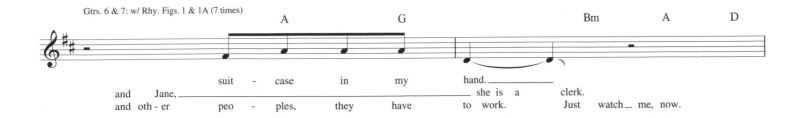

Gtrs. 6 & 7: w/ Rhy. Figs. 1 & 1A (7 times)

suit - case in my hand.
and Jane,_____ she is a clerk.
and oth - er peo - ples, they have to work. Just watch__ me, now.

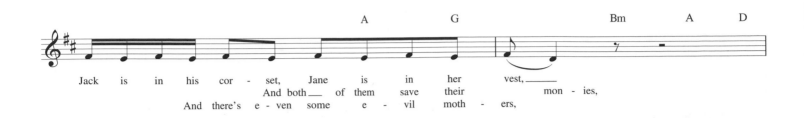

Jack is in his cor - set, Jane is in her vest,____
And both__ of them save their mon - ies,
And there's e - ven some e - vil moth - ers,

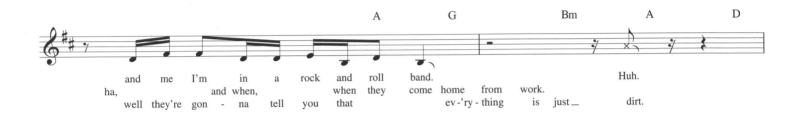

and me I'm in a rock and roll band. Huh.
ha, and when, when they come home from work.
well they're gon - na tell you that ev -'ry - thing is just__ dirt.

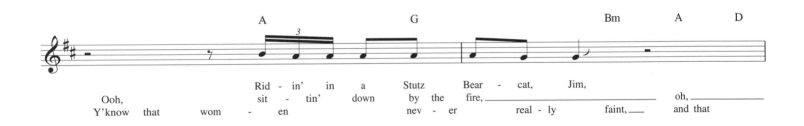

Ooh, Rid - in' in a Stutz Bear - cat, Jim, oh,_____
Y'know that wom - en nev - er real - ly faint,___ and that

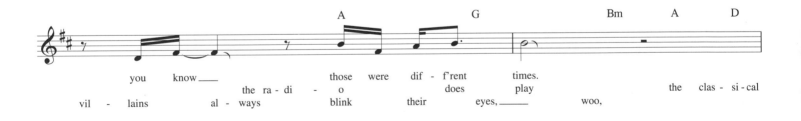

you know____ those were dif - f'rent times.
vil - lains al - ways blink their eyes,___ woo, the clas - si - cal
the ra - di - o does play

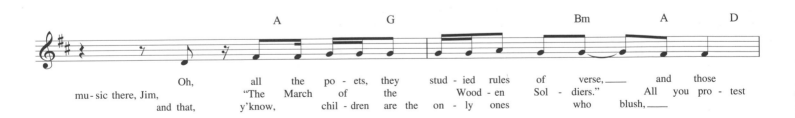

Oh, all the po - ets, they stud - ied rules of verse,____ and those
mu - sic there, Jim, "The March of the Wood - en Sol - diers." All you pro - test
and that, y'know, chil - dren are the on - ly ones who blush,___

3rd time, To Coda ⊕

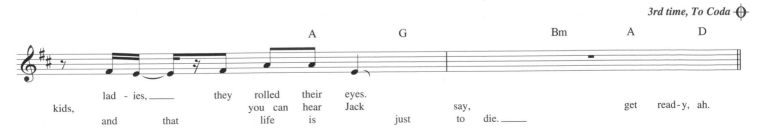

lad - ies,___ they rolled their eyes.
kids, you can hear Jack say, get read - y, ah.
and that life is just to die.___

244

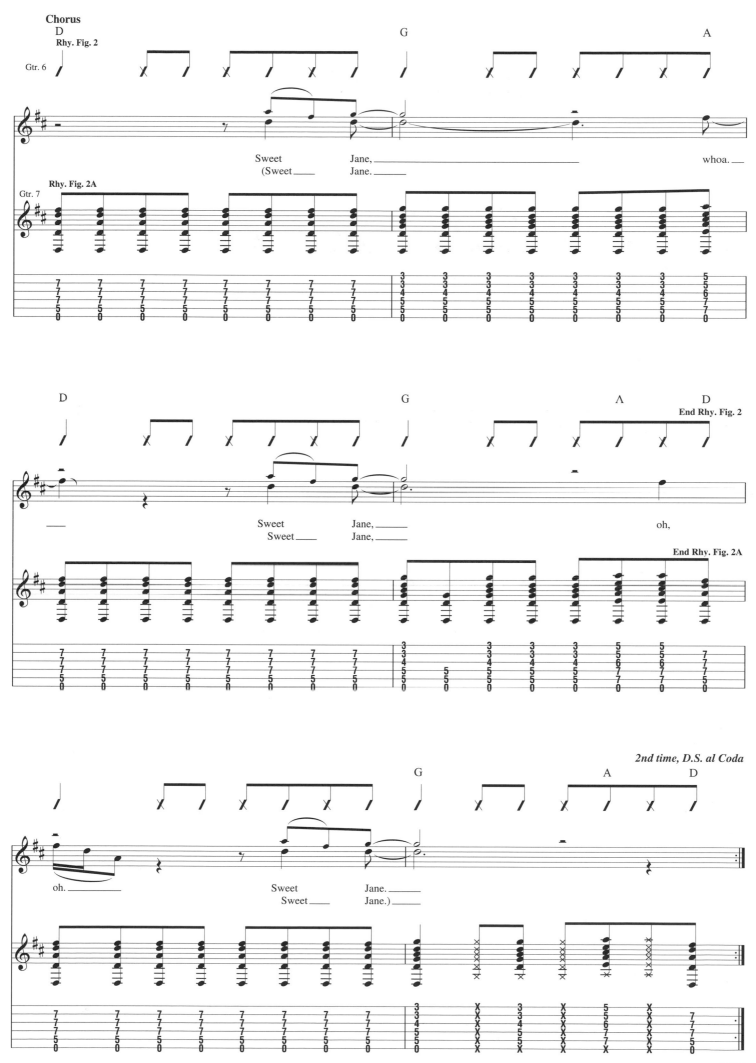

⊕ **Coda**

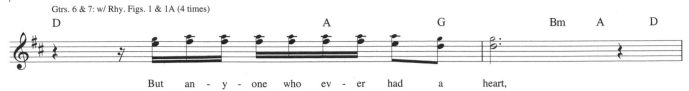

But an - y - one who ev - er had a heart,

oh, they would - n't turn a - round and break it.

And an - y - one who ev - er played a part,

oh, they would - n't turn a - round and hate it.

Chorus

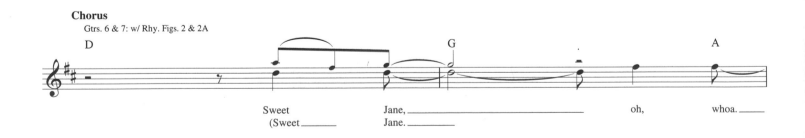

Sweet Jane, oh, whoa.
(Sweet Jane.

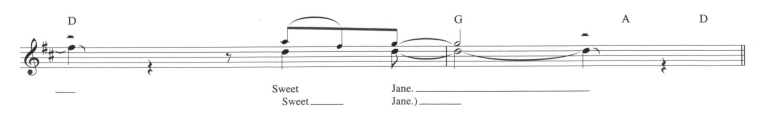

Sweet Jane.
Sweet Jane.)

Outro

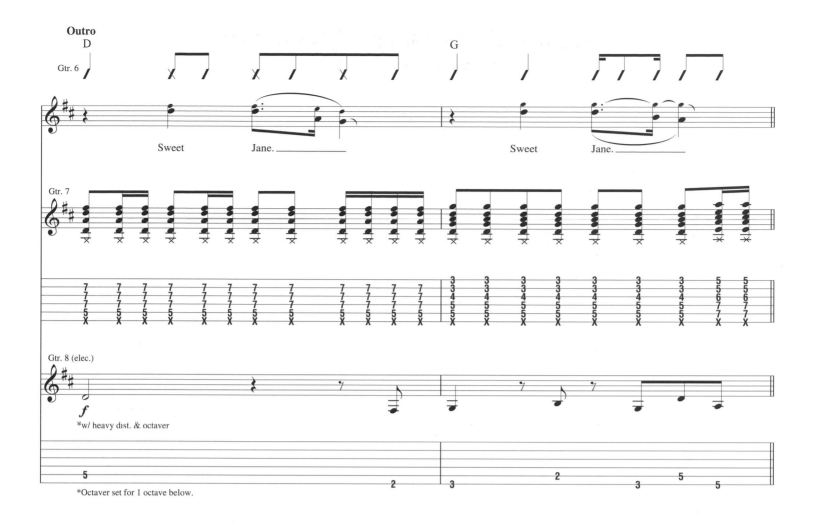

*Octaver set for 1 octave below.

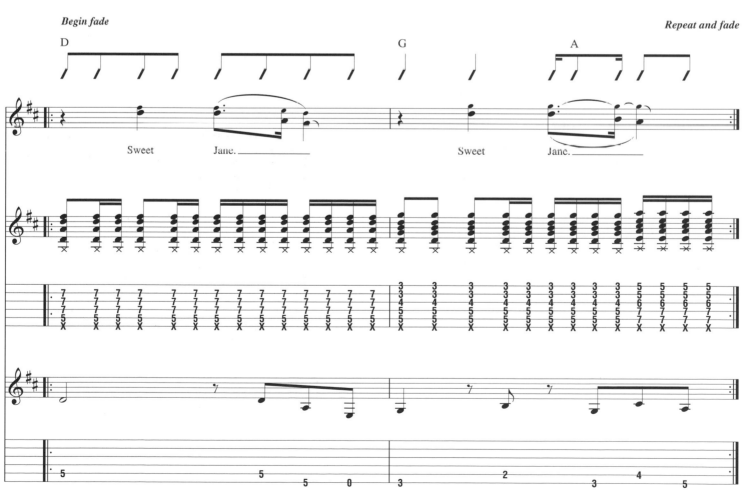

Sweet Talkin' Woman

Words and Music by Jeff Lynne

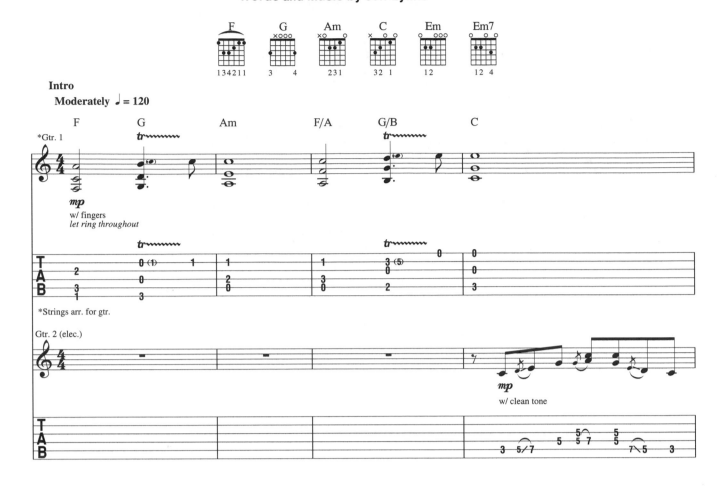

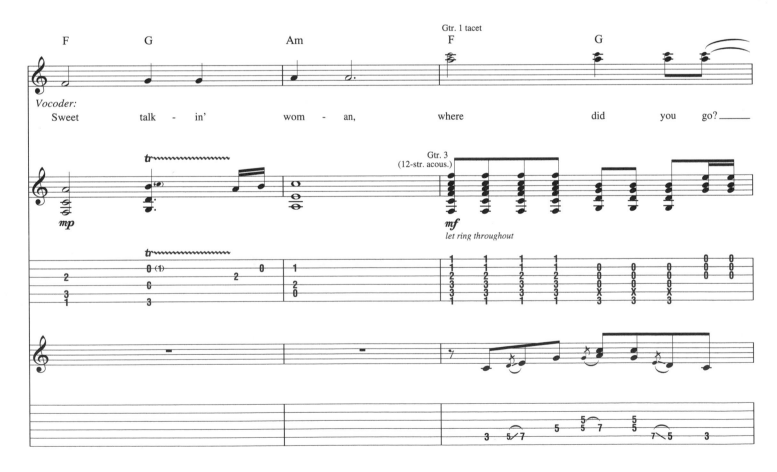

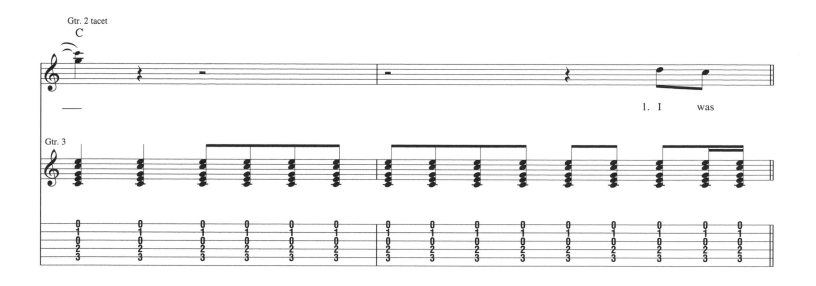

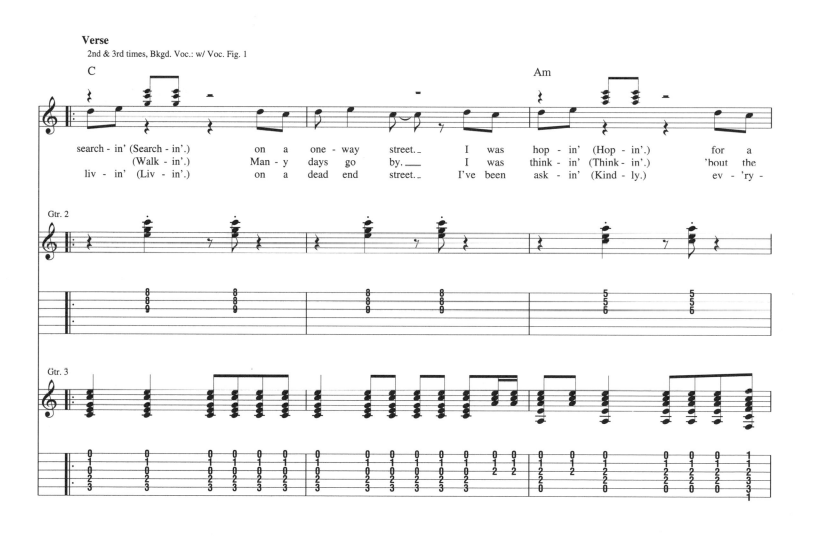

chance to ___ meet. ___ I was wait-in' for the op – er - a – tor on the line. ___
lone - ly nights. ___ Com - mu - ni - ca - tion ___ break - down all a - round. ___
bod - y I meet. In – suf - fi – cient da – ta com - in' through. ___

Pre-Chorus

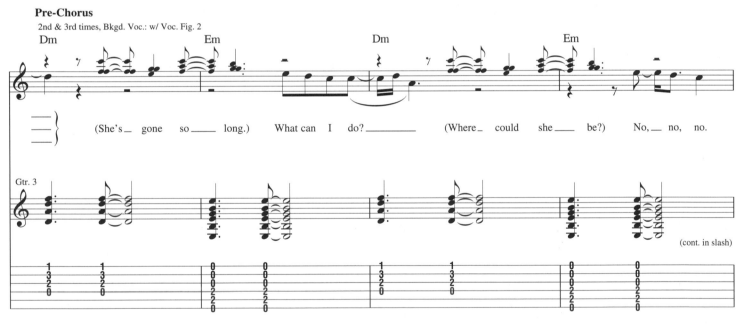

2nd & 3rd times, Bkgd. Voc.: w/ Voc. Fig. 2

(She's ___ gone so ___ long.) What can I do? ___ (Where ___ could she ___ be?) No, ___ no, no.

(cont. in slash)

Voc. Fig. 2

(Hey, hey, hey, hey, hey, hey, hey, hey.)

(Duh dup, duh dup, duh dup, duh dup, duh dup, duh dup.)

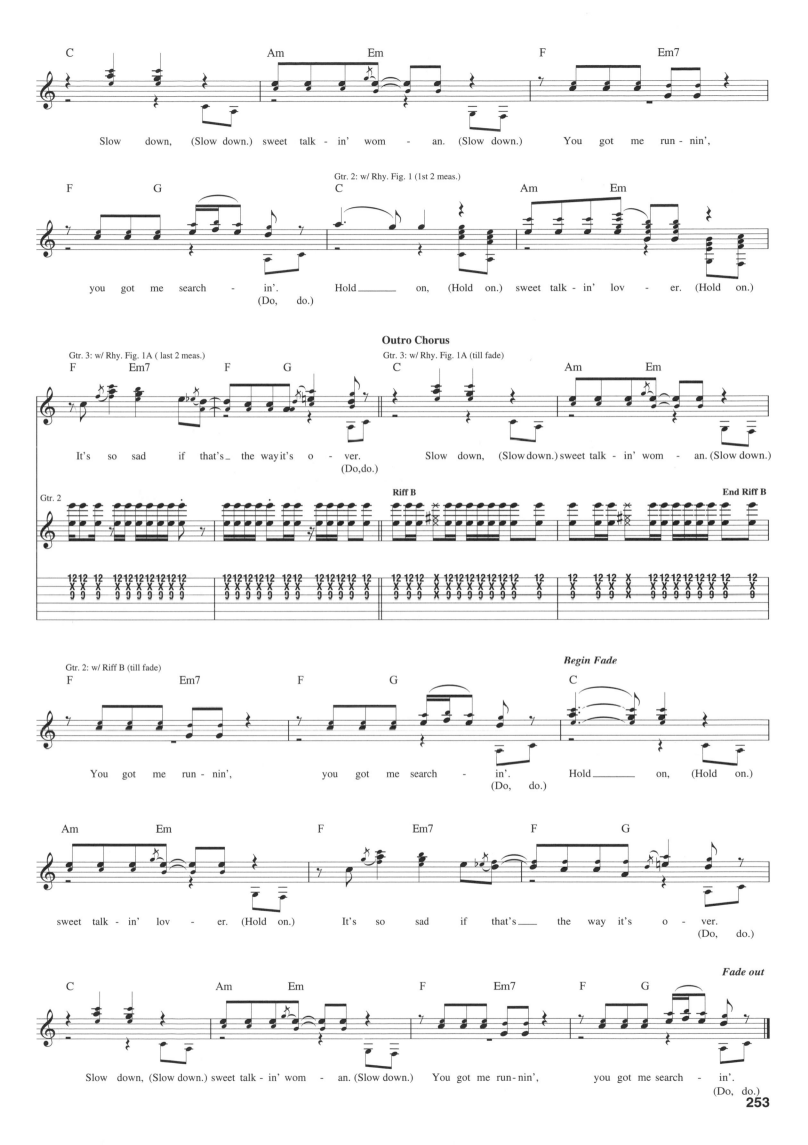

3 AM

Lyrics by Rob Thomas

Music by Rob Thomas, Brian Yale, John Leslie Goff and John Joseph Stanley

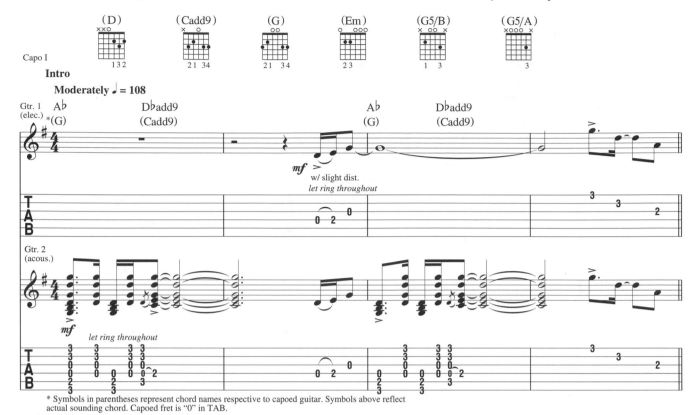

* Symbols in parentheses represent chord names respective to capoed guitar. Symbols above reflect actual sounding chord. Capoed fret is "0" in TAB.

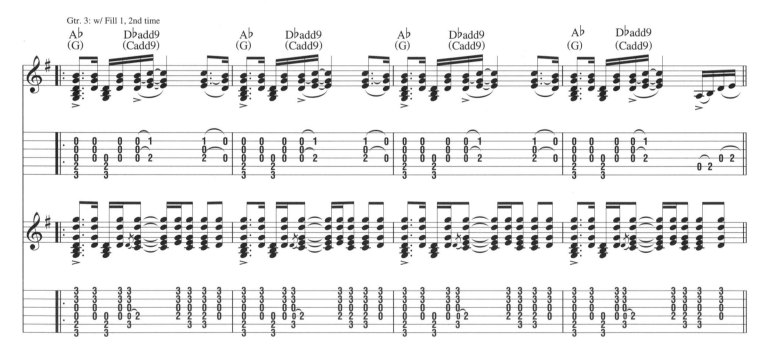

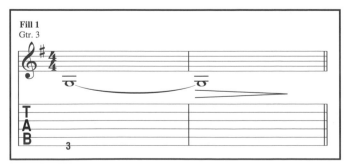

Verse

Gtr. 2: w/ Rhy. Fig. 1C, 3 times, 2nd time

1. She says it's cold _____ out - side _____ and she hands _____ me my rain
2. But she's gotta lit - tle _____ bit of _____ some - thin', _____ God, it's bet - ter than noth -

* Turn on tremolo effect during 3rd & 4th meas. of Rhy. Fig. 1B

_____ coat.
- in'.

255

Gtr. 1: w/ Rhy. Fig. 1, 1 3/4 times
Gtr. 2: w/ Rhy. Fig. 1A, 2 times, 1st time
Gtr. 3: w/ Rhy. Fig. 1B, 2 times

She's al - ways wor - ried a - bout _ things _ like _ that. _
And in her col - or por - trait world she be - lieves that she's got it all, _____ all.

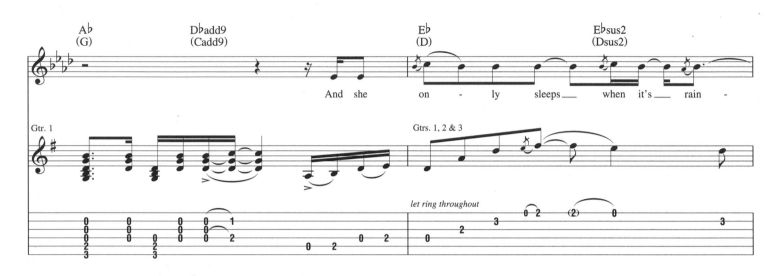

Well, she says it's all _ gon - na end _ and it might as _ well be my _ fault. }
She swears the moon _ don't hang _ quite as _ high _ as it used to. }

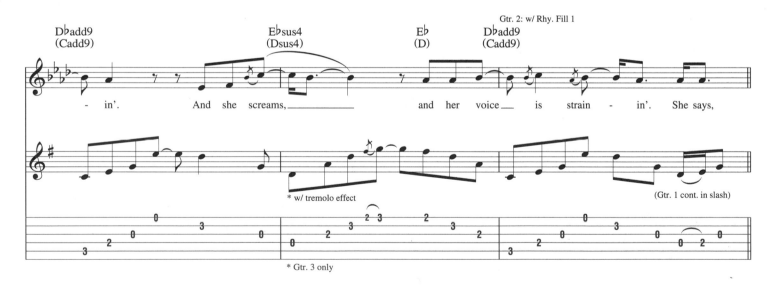

And she on - ly sleeps _ when it's _ rain -

Gtr. 1

Gtrs. 1, 2 & 3

let ring throughout

Gtr. 2: w/ Rhy. Fill 1

- in'. And she screams, _____ and her voice _ is strain - in'. She says,

* w/ tremolo effect

(Gtr. 1 cont. in slash)

* Gtr. 3 only

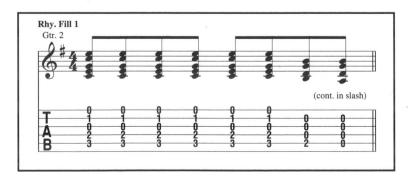

Rhy. Fill 1

Gtr. 2

(cont. in slash)

rain's gon-na wash a-way, ___ I be - lieve, ___ yes. ___

(cont. in slash)

Interlude

Verse

Gtrs. 2 & 3: w/ Rhy. Figs. 1A & 1B, 3 times

3. Well, she be-lieves_ that life_ is made up of all_ that you're used_ to.

Gtr. 1

And the clock on the wall_____ has_ been stuck at three_ for

days_ and days._ She thinks that hap-

Harm. - - - - - - - - - - - - - - - -

- pi - ness_ is a mat_ that sits_ on her door - way,_____ yeah. But

Harm. - - - - - -

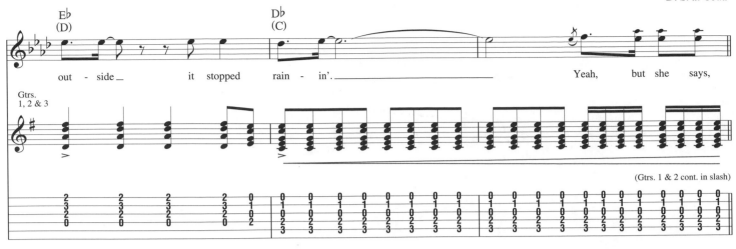

out - side ___ it stopped rain - in'. ___ Yeah, but she says,

Coda

___ some - times." ___ And the rain's gon - na wash a - way, ___ I be - lieve

w/ clean tone
let ring throughout

Outro

Gtrs. 1 & 2: w/ Rhy. Fig. 2, 3 times
Gtr. 3: w/ Rhy. Fig. 3

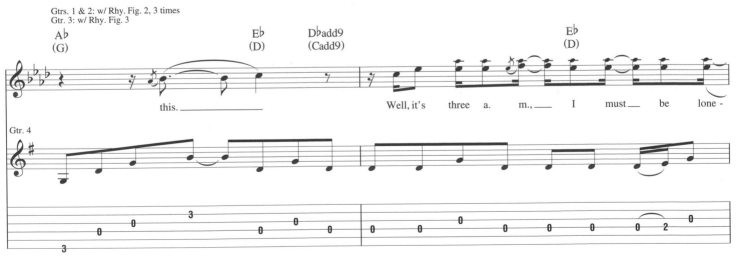

this. ___ Well, it's three a. m., ___ I must ___ be lone -

Gtr. 4

Wherever You Will Go

Words and Music by Aaron Kamin and Alex Band

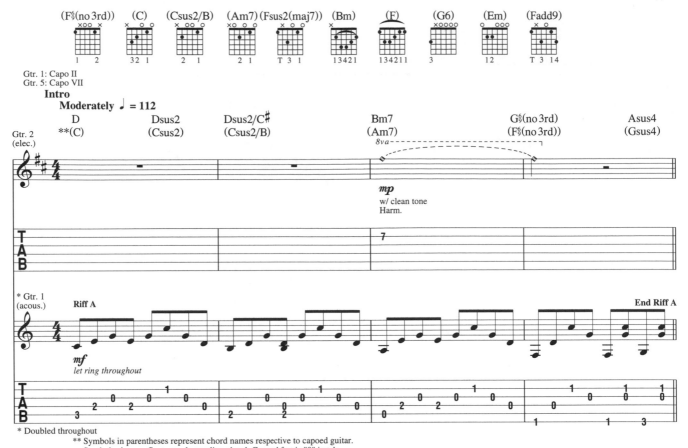

Gtr. 1: Capo II
Gtr. 5: Capo VII

Intro
Moderately ♩ = 112

* Doubled throughout
** Symbols in parentheses represent chord names respective to capoed guitar.
Symbols above reflect actual sounding chord. Capoed fret is "0" in tab.

Verse

Gtr. 1: w/ Riff A (3 times)
Gtr. 2 tacet

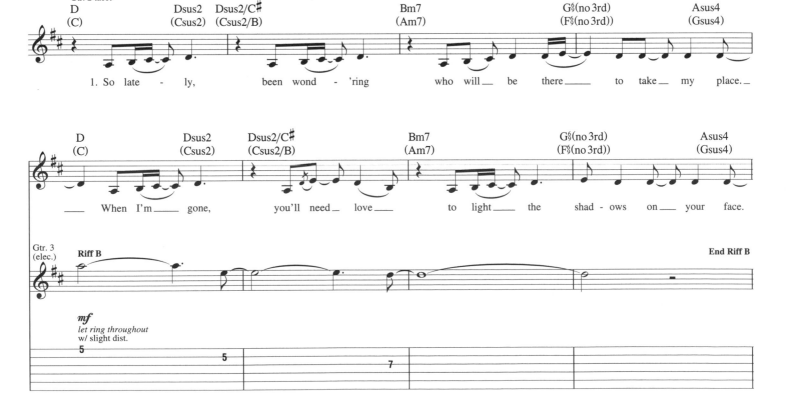

1. So late - ly, been wond - 'ring who will __ be there __ to take __ my place. __

__ When I'm __ gone, you'll need __ love __ to light __ the shad - ows on your face.

Verse

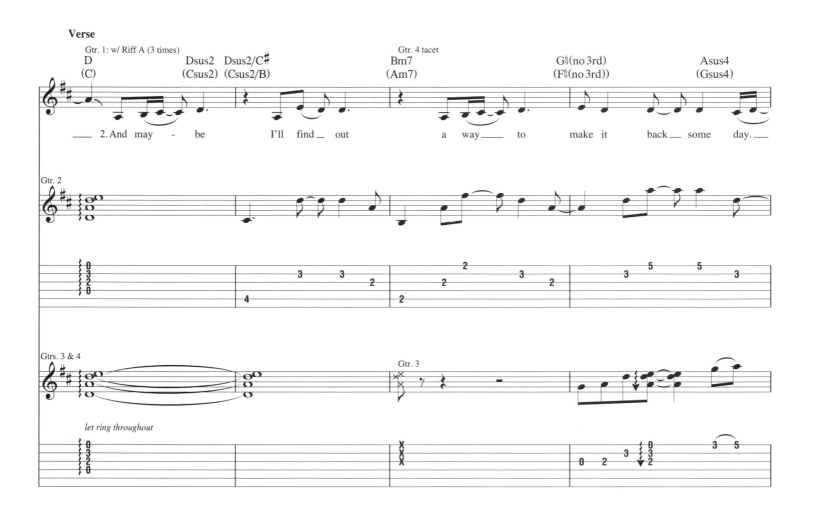

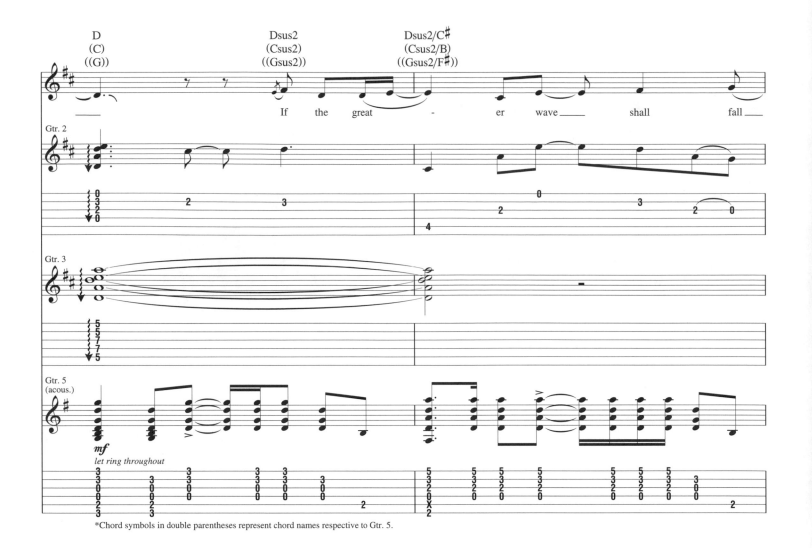

*Chord symbols in double parentheses represent chord names respective to Gtr. 5.

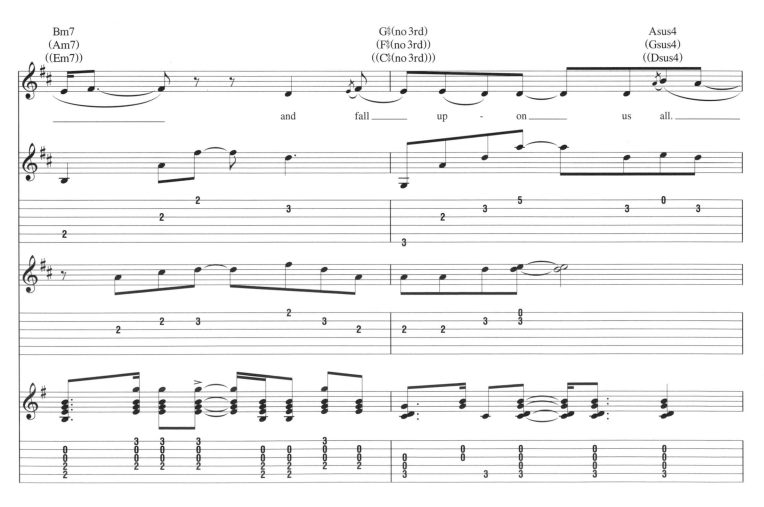

Verse

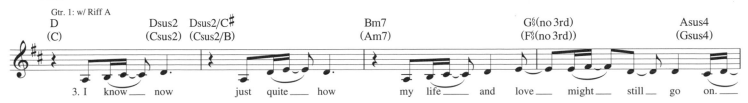

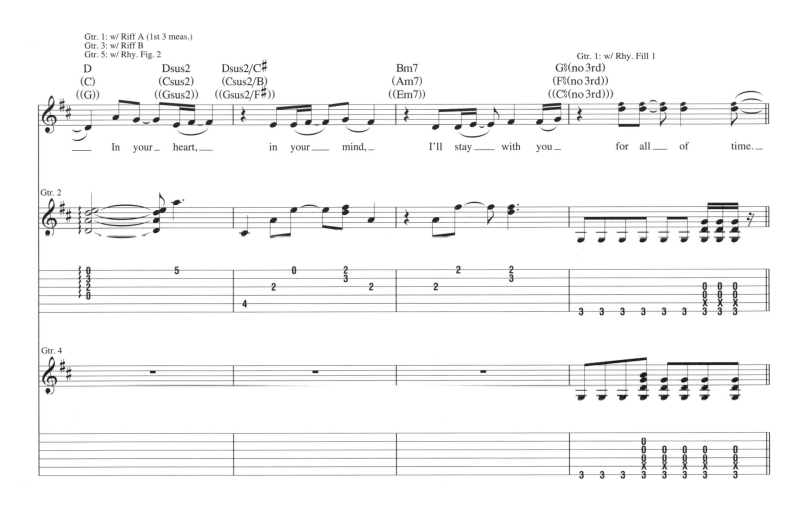

Chorus

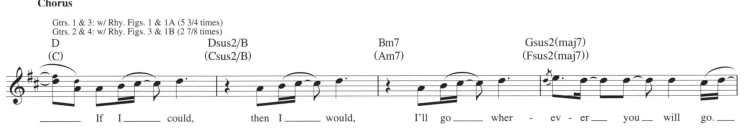

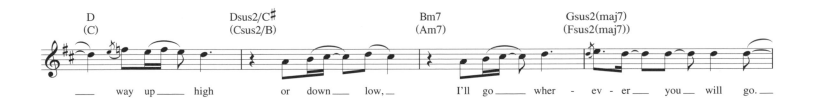

Guitar Notation Legend

Guitar Music can be notated three different ways: on a *musical staff*, in *tablature*, and in *rhythm slashes*.

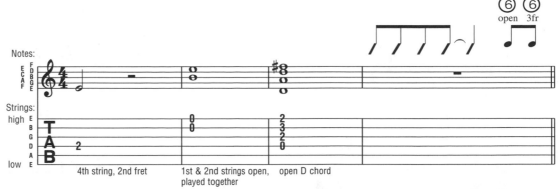

RHYTHM SLASHES are written above the staff. Strum chords in the rhythm indicated. Use the chord diagrams found at the top of the first page of the transcription for the appropriate chord voicings. Round noteheads indicate single notes.

THE MUSICAL STAFF shows pitches and rhythms and is divided by bar lines into measures. Pitches are named after the first seven letters of the alphabet.

TABLATURE graphically represents the guitar fingerboard. Each horizontal line represents a string, and each number represents a fret.

HALF-STEP BEND: Strike the note and bend up 1/2 step.

WHOLE-STEP BEND: Strike the note and bend up one step.

GRACE NOTE BEND: Strike the note and immediately bend up as indicated.

SLIGHT (MICROTONE) BEND: Strike the note and bend up 1/4 step.

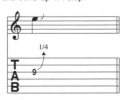

BEND AND RELEASE: Strike the note and bend up as indicated, then release back to the original note. Only the first note is struck.

PRE-BEND: Bend the note as indicated, then strike it.

VIBRATO: The string is vibrated by rapidly bending and releasing the note with the fretting hand.

WIDE VIBRATO: The pitch is varied to a greater degree by vibrating with the fretting hand.

HAMMER-ON: Strike the first (lower) note with one finger, then sound the higher note (on the same string) with another finger by fretting it without picking.

PULL-OFF: Place both fingers on the notes to be sounded. Strike the first note and without picking, pull the finger off to sound the second (lower) note.

LEGATO SLIDE: Strike the first note and then slide the same fret-hand finger up or down to the second note. The second note is not struck.

SHIFT SLIDE: Same as legato slide, except the second note is struck.

TRILL: Very rapidly alternate between the notes indicated by continuously hammering on and pulling off.

TAPPING: Hammer ("tap") the fret indicated with the pick-hand index or middle finger and pull off to the note fretted by the fret hand.

NATURAL HARMONIC: Strike the note while the fret-hand lightly touches the string directly over the fret indicated.

PINCH HARMONIC: The note is fretted normally and a harmonic is produced by adding the edge of the thumb or the tip of the index finger of the pick hand to the normal pick attack.

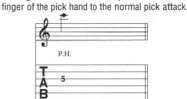

PICK SCRAPE: The edge of the pick is rubbed down (or up) the string, producing a scratchy sound.

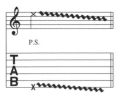

MUFFLED STRINGS: A percussive sound is produced by laying the fret hand across the string(s) without depressing, and striking them with the pick hand.

PALM MUTING: The note is partially muted by the pick hand lightly touching the string(s) just before the bridge.

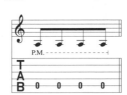

RAKE: Drag the pick across the strings indicated with a single motion.

TREMOLO PICKING: The note is picked as rapidly and continuously as possible.

VIBRATO BAR DIVE AND RETURN: The pitch of the note or chord is dropped a specified number of steps (in rhythm) then returned to the original pitch.

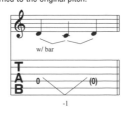

VIBRATO BAR SCOOP: Depress the bar just before striking the note, then quickly release the bar.

VIBRATO BAR DIP: Strike the note and then immediately drop a specified number of steps, then release back to the original pitch.

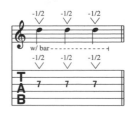

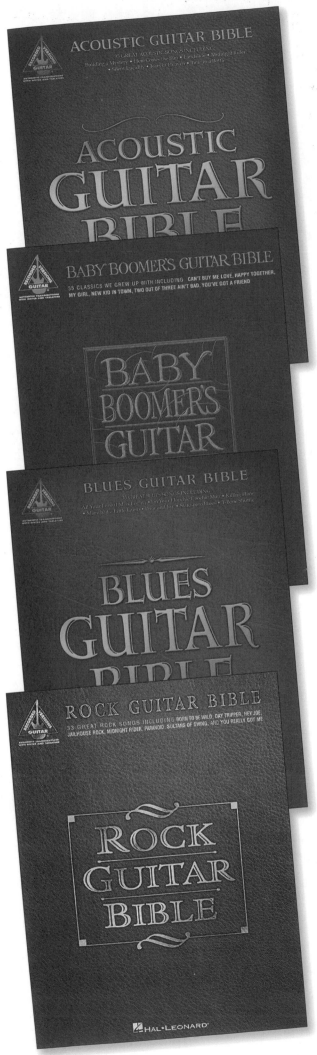

GUITAR BIBLES

from

Hal Leonard proudly presents the Guitar Bible series.
Each volume contains great songs in authentic,
note-for-note transcriptions with lyrics and tablature. $19.95 each

ACOUSTIC GUITAR BIBLE
35 acoustic classics: Angie • Building a Mystery • Change the World • Dust in the Wind • Here Comes the Sun • Hold My Hand • Iris • Maggie May • Southern Cross • Tears in Heaven • Wild World • You Were Meant for Me • and more.
_____00690432..................................$19.95

BABY BOOMER'S GUITAR BIBLE
35 songs: Angie • Can't Buy Me Love • Happy Together • Hey Jude • Imagine • Laughing • Longer • My Girl • New Kid in Town • Rebel, Rebel • Wild Thing • and more.
_____00690412..................................$19.95

BLUES GUITAR BIBLE
35 blues tunes: Boom Boom • Everyday (I Have the Blues) • Hide Away • I Can't Quit You Baby • I'm Your Hoochie Coochie Man • Killing Floor • Pride and Joy • Sweet Little Angel • The Thrill Is Gone • and more.
_____00690437..................................$19.95

BLUES-ROCK GUITAR BIBLE
35 songs: Cross Road Blues (Crossroads) • Hide Away • The House Is Rockin' • Love Struck Baby • Move It On Over • Piece of My Heart • Statesboro Blues • You Shook Me • more.
_____00690450..................................$19.95

COUNTRY GUITAR BIBLE
35 country classics: Ain't Goin' Down ('Til the Sun Comes Up) • Blue Eyes Crying in the Rain • Boot Scootin' Boogie • Friends in Low Places • I'm So Lonesome I Could Cry • T-R-O-U-B-L-E • and more.
_____00690465..................................$19.95

FOLK-ROCK GUITAR BIBLE
35 songs: At Seventeen • Blackbird • Fire and Rain • Happy Together • Leaving on a Jet Plane • Our House • Time in a Bottle • Turn! Turn! Turn! • You've Got a Friend • more.
_____00690464..................................$19.95

HARD ROCK GUITAR BIBLE
35 songs: Ballroom Blitz • Bang a Gong • Barracuda • Living After Midnight • Rock You like a Hurricane • School's Out • Welcome to the Jungle • You Give Love a Bad Name • more.
_____00690453..................................$19.95

INSTRUMENTAL GUITAR BIBLE
37 great instrumentals: Always with Me, Always with You • Big Foot • The Claw • Cliffs of Dover • For the Love of God • Frankenstein • Freeway Jam • Green Onions • Hide Away • Jessica • Lenny • Linus and Lucy • Perfidia • Pipeline • Raunchy • Rawhide • Rebel 'Rouser • Rumble • Satch Boogie • Scuttle Buttin' • Sleepwalk • The Stumble • T-Bone Shuffle • Tequila • Walk Don't Run • Wham • and more.
_____00690514..................................$19.95

JAZZ GUITAR BIBLE
31 songs: Body and Soul • In a Sentimental Mood • My Funny Valentine • Nuages • Satin Doll • So What • Star Dust • Take Five • Tangerine • Yardbird Suite • and more.
_____00690466..................................$19.95

NU METAL GUITAR BIBLE
25 edgy metal hits: Aenema • Black • Edgecrusher • Last Resort • People of the Sun • Schism • Sleep Now in the Fire • Southtown • Take a Look Around • Toxicity • Your Disease • Youth of the Nation • and more.
_____00690569..................................$19.95

POP/ROCK GUITAR BIBLE
35 pop hits: Change the World • Heartache Tonight • Hold My Hand • Money for Nothing • Mony, Mony • More Than Words • Pink Houses • Smooth • Summer of '69 • 3 AM • What I Like About You • and more.
_____00690517..................................$19.95

R&B GUITAR BIBLE
35 R&B classics: Brick House • Fire • I Got You (I Feel Good) • Love Rollercoaster • Shining Star • Sir Duke • Super Freak • and more.
_____00690452..................................$19.95

ROCK GUITAR BIBLE
33 songs: All Day and All of the Night • Born to Be Wild • Day Tripper • Gloria • Hey Joe • Jailhouse Rock • Money • Paranoid • Sultans of Swing • Walk This Way • You Really Got Me • more!
_____00690313..................................$19.95

ROCKABILLY GUITAR BIBLE
30 songs from artists such as Elvis, Buddy Holly and the Brian Setzer Orchestra: Blue Suede Shoes • Hello Mary Lou • Peggy Sue • Rock This Town • Travelin' Man • and more.
_____00690570..................................$19.95

SOUL GUITAR BIBLE
33 songs: Groovin' • I've Been Loving You Too Long • Let's Get It On • My Girl • Respect • Theme from Shaft • Soul Man • and more.
_____00690506..................................$19.95

FOR MORE INFORMATION, SEE YOUR LOCAL MUSIC DEALER,
OR WRITE TO:

HAL•LEONARD®
CORPORATION

7777 W. BLUEMOUND RD. P.O. BOX 13819 MILWAUKEE, WI 53213

Prices, contents, and availability subject to change without notice.

www.halleonard.com

0903